Ludwig II.

Ludwig II of Bavaria
Louis II de Bavière

Hans F. Nöhbauer

TASCHEN

KÖLN LISBOA LONDON NEW YORK PARIS TOKYO

Cover:
The Young King in General's Uniform with Coronation Cloak
Painting by Karl Piloty, 1865

Back cover:
Neuschwanstein Castle

Front flap:
Ludwig II's bedroom in Herrenchiemsee

Inner front flap:
Herrenchiemsee Castle

Back flap:
Majolica flower vase in the shape of a swan

Inner back flap:
Hohenschwangau Castle with Lakes Alp and Schwan

Illustration page 2:
Ludwig II as Grand Master of the Royal Order of the Knights of Saint George
Painting by Georg Papperitz, 1901

© 1998 Benedikt Taschen Verlag GmbH
Hohenzollernring 53, D–50672 Köln

English translation: Christian Goodden, Bungay (UK)
French translation: Michèle Schreyer, Cologne
Edited by Michael Konze und Petra Hugenschmidt, Cologne
Cover Design: Claudia Frey, Cologne

Printed in Portugal
ISBN 3–8228–7430–2

Inhalt | Content | Sommaire

Kindheit

Childhood

Das freudige Ereignis brachte die Einwohner der königlichen Haupt- und Residenzstadt München um ihren Schlaf. Denn morgens um drei verkündeten 25 Kanonenschüsse, daß dem Kronprinzen Maximilian an diesem 25. August 1845 ein Erbe geboren worden war. So schrieb der Verfasser des „Bayerischen Wörterbuches" Johann Andreas Schmeller in sein Tagebuch. Oder hatte die Artillerie vielleicht doch 101 Salutschüsse abgegeben, wie die Mutter des Neugeborenen, Prinzessin Marie, an ihre Familie in Berlin schrieb?

Am Abend des vorangegangenen Tages war König Ludwig I. aus seiner Residenz nach Schloß Nymphenburg gefahren, hatte dort mit der Uhr in der Hand auf einem Sofa gesessen und beobachtet, wie der Zeiger sich immer weiter gegen Mitternacht bewegte – und kurz nachdem der neue Tag, sein 59. Geburts- und zugleich sein Namenstag, angebrochen war, erhielt er die Nachricht, daß er Großvater geworden sei.

Im nachhinein wurde heimlich getuschelt, daß der spätere König Ludwig II. in Wirklichkeit bereits einige Tage früher zur Welt gekommen sei, daß man aber die Nachricht zurückgehalten habe, um dem alten Herrn (den die Tänzerin Lola Montez gut zweieinhalb Jahre später um den Thron bringen sollte) den Enkel gleichsam als Geburtstagsgeschenk zu präsentieren.

Drei Jahrzehnte später, inzwischen selbst schon viele Jahre König, schrieb Ludwig II. der Schauspielerin Marie Dahn-Hausmann den seither oft zitierten Satz: „Ein ewig Räthsel bleiben will ich mir und anderen." Der Anfang dieses Rätsels liegt also bereits in seiner Geburt.

Dem pompösen, einem künftigen König angemessenen Empfang mit lautem Kanonendonner folgte eine Kindheit, wie sie kärglicher und wohl auch liebloser kaum erahnt werden kann. Der Vater, seit einer Typhuserkrankung immer ein wenig geschwächt und unter Kopfschmerzen leidend, wollte seine beiden Söhne Ludwig und den mehr als zwei Jahre jüngeren Otto von Kindestagen an die Bürde königlicher Pflichten lehren. Das Taschengeld wurde in wenigen kleinen Münzen gezahlt, und das Essen war so dürftig, daß sich die Magd Lisi

Childhood

In Munich, the capital and royal seat, the happy event robbed the inhabitants of their sleep. For at three o'clock in the morning cannons sounded off a 25-gun salute to announce that on this day, 25 August 1845, an heir had been born to Crown Prince Maximilian. Such was the diary entry of Johann Andreas Schmeller, the author of the "Bavarian Dictionary". Or perhaps, after all, the artillery had fired off a 101-gun salute, as the mother of the newborn, Princess Marie, wrote to her family in Berlin.

The previous evening, King Ludwig I had driven out from his residence to Nymphenburg Castle, where – watch in hand – he had sat on a sofa observing the hour hand as it moved inexorably towards midnight, and shortly after the new day, his 59th birthday and name day, had broken, he received word that he had become a grandfather.

Afterwards it was whispered secretly that the future King Ludwig II had actually come into the world a few days earlier, but that the news had been suppressed so as to make the grandson a kind of birthday present for the old man (whom the dancer Lola Montez was to do out of the throne a good two-and-a-half years later).

Three decades later, Ludwig II, himself now king for a number of years, wrote to the actress Marie Dahn-Hausmann the much-quoted sentence: "I want to remain an eternal enigma both to myself and others." The seeds of the enigma were, it seems, already sown at his birth.

If the new arrival was greeted with a booming grandiose reception fit for a future king, his subsequent childhood could hardly have been more meagre or unloving. His father, a sickly man plagued by headaches since an attack of typhoid, wanted to instruct his two sons Ludwig and Otto (the latter was more than two years younger than his brother Ludwig) in the burdens of royal duty from their childhood onwards. Their pocket money comprised just a few small coins, and their food was so paltry that the maid Lisi sometimes crept into the room of the two princes to give them morsels from the servants' kitchen. His Majesty, who

L'enfance

La bonne nouvelle priva les habitants de Munich de sommeil. En effet, ce 25 août 1845 à trois heures du matin, vingt-cinq coups de canon annoncèrent dans la capitale de la Bavière qu'un fils était né au prince héritier Maximilien. C'est du moins ce qu'écrivit Johann Andreas Schmeller, le rédacteur du « Dictionnaire bavarois », dans son journal intime. La princesse Marie, la mère du nouveau-né, en avait un tout autre souvenir : elle fit en effet savoir à sa famille vivant à Berlin que l'artillerie avait tiré cent et un coups pour saluer cette naissance.

La veille au soir, le roi Louis Ier (il abdiquera un peu plus de deux ans et demi plus tard, la danseuse Lola Montez lui ayant été fatale) avait quitté sa résidence pour le palais de Nymphenbourg. Là, assis sur un canapé, il avait observé les aiguilles de sa montre se diriger inexorablement vers minuit – et peu après la venue du jour nouveau, celui de son anniversaire et de son saint patron, il apprit qu'il était devenu grand-père.

Plus tard, on murmurera en cachette que le futur Louis II avait vu le jour plusieurs jours auparavant, mais que l'on avait gardé la nouvelle secrète pour offrir au souverain un petit-fils comme cadeau d'anniversaire.

Une trentaine d'années plus tard, il régnait alors lui-même depuis de nombreuses années, Louis II écrivit à la comédienne Marie Dahn-Hausmann la phrase souvent citée depuis : « Je veux rester pour moi-même et les autres une énigme éternelle. » On le voit, le jour de sa naissance est déjà placé sous le signe du mystère.

L'accueil pompeux et sonore, digne d'un futur souverain, qu'il reçut en ce monde, fut suivi d'une enfance que l'on ne saurait imaginer plus démunie sur le plan affectif. Le père, qui ne s'était jamais remis du typhus, restant affaibli et souffrant de maux de tête, voulait que ses fils Louis et Othon – ce dernier étant le cadet, connaissent dès leur plus jeune âge les fardeaux qui incombent au monarque. L'argent de poche se résumait à un peu de petite monnaie, et la nourriture était si frugale que la servante Lisi se glissait à l'occasion dans la chambre des princes pour leur apporter à manger de la table des domestiques. Sa Majesté – montée sur le trône au printemps 1848 sous le nom de Maximilien II – avait

Fünf Jahre alt und wie ein Mädchen gekleidet: Kronprinz Ludwig mit seinen Eltern und Bruder Otto 1850 in Hohenschwangau.

Five years old and dressed like a girl: Crown Prince Ludwig with his parents and brother Otto in 1850 at Hohenschwangau.

Cinq ans et vêtu comme une fille : le prince héritier Louis avec ses parents et son frère Othon en 1850 à Hohenschwangau.

Die Prinzen Ludwig und Otto in ihren offensichtlich zu groß geratenen Trachtenanzügen
vor Schloß Hohenschwangau.

Princes Ludwig and Otto in front of Hohenschwangau Castle, wearing traditional
national loden suits that seem a little on the
large size!

Les princes Louis et Othon dans des costumes
manifestement trop grands pour eux devant le
château de Hohenschwangau.

Königin Marie mit ihren beiden Söhnen Ludwig und Otto am Alpsee bei Hohenschwangau,
gemalt von Ernst Rietschel im Jahre 1850.

Queen Marie with her two sons Ludwig and
Otto at Lake Alp near Hohenschwangau,
painted in 1850 by Ernst Rietschel.

La reine Marie et ses deux fils Louis et Othon
au lac de Alp près de Hohenschwangau, peints
par Ernst Rietschel en 1850.

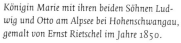

Der 20-jährige König Ludwig II., aufgenommen vom Hofphotographen Joseph Albert
im Jahre 1865.

The twenty-year-old King Ludwig II, taken
in 1865 by court photographer Joseph Albert.

Louis II à vingt ans, photographié en 1865 par
Joseph Albert.

Die wittelsbachischen Brüder. Ludwig hält in der Hand ein Skizzenbuch, in das er 1853 das Schloß Hohenschwangau zeichnete.

The Wittelsbach brothers. Ludwig is holding a sketchbook in which in 1853 he drew Hohenschwangau Castle.

Les frères de Wittelsbach. Louis tient un carnet de croquis dans lequel il dessine le château de Hohenschwangau en 1853.

gelegentlich in das Zimmer der beiden Prinzen schlich, um sie aus der Dienstbotenküche zu versorgen. Weil Ludwigs Vater – seit dem Frühjahr 1848 regierte er unter dem Namen Maximilian II. – eine so hohe Meinung von der Würde seines Hauses hatte, untersagte er den Söhnen den Umgang mit anderen Kindern.

Dabei meinte es der griesgrämige, melancholische König sicher gut, doch indem er Ludwig und Otto nach seinem Bild formen wollte, verloren die Prinzen den Bezug zur Wirklichkeit.

Als Ludwig seinen achtzehnten Geburtstag und damit seine Volljährigkeit feierte, bekam er von seinem Vater einen Beutel mit Münzen geschenkt, die alle in Bayern gültigen Geldstücke repräsentierten. Da Ludwig an den Umgang mit Geld kaum gewöhnt war, dachte er, er könne damit ein Medaillon für seine Mutter kaufen, wurde aber bitter enttäuscht, da es bei weitem nicht für solch ein wertvolles Schmuckstück ausreichte. Seit diesem Erlebnis, sagt man, habe sich Ludwig nie mehr für den Wert des Geldes interessiert.

Es gab aber immer wieder Forscher, die weniger der falschen Erziehung als der Vererbung die Schuld am tragischen Schicksal der beiden Königssöhne geben. Bei den Wittelsbachern, meinen sie, sei keine Degeneration festzustellen, „das explosive Hervortreten zweier geisteskranker Brüder [sei] lediglich dem Umstande zuzuschreiben, daß ein schwächlicher Vertreter der wittelsbacher Dynastie in dem vereinigten hohenzollerisch-braunschweigerischem Blute seiner Frau höchst unglückliche Ergänzung fand". Die Ursache der Geistesverwirrung bei Ludwig und Otto will man schließlich bei einem 1535 geborenen Herzog Wilhelm dem Jüngeren von Braunschweig gefunden haben.

So wäre der Fall geklärt. Die Freunde und Verehrer König Ludwigs gehen aber davon aus (und haben dafür auch Gründe), daß ihr Märchenkönig zwar von schwerem Gemüt, doch keineswegs geisteskrank gewesen sei.

since the spring of 1848 had ruled under the name of Maximilian II, had such a high opinion of the dignity of his house that he forbade his sons to associate with other children.

No doubt the grumpy melancholic king meant well, but by wanting to mould Ludwig and Otto in his own image, he caused the two princes to lose touch with reality.

When Ludwig celebrated his eighteenth birthday and thereby reached adulthood, his father gave him a purse containing all the different coins which were legal tender in Bavaria. As Ludwig had had very little experience with money, he naïvely believed he could buy a locket for his mother with the contents of the purse. On discovering this was totally insufficient to buy such a valuable piece of jewellery, he suffered a bitter disappointment. From that day on, it is said, Ludwig never again showed the slightest interest in the value of money.

Despite this circumstance, numerous researchers have attributed the blame for the two princes' tragic fate not so much to their misguided upbringing, but more to hereditary considerations. Although, they maintain, there is no trace of degeneracy in the Wittelsbach line itself, "the sudden appearance of two mentally disturbed brothers can be explained by the fact that a weakly representative of the Wittelsbach dynasty made a highly unfortunate genetic match in his wife's combined Hohenzollern-Brunswick blood." Ultimately, so they claim, the cause of Ludwig and Otto's mental confusion can be traced back to one Wilhelm the Younger Duke of Brunswick, born in 1535.

And there the matter would rest, except that friends and admirers of King Ludwig are compelled to counter (not without reasons of their own) that their fairytale king may have been of a brooding disposition, but was by no means mentally unhinged.

une si haute idée de la grandeur de sa maison, qu'Elle interdisait à Ses fils de fréquenter les autres enfants.

Le roi mélancolique et bougon avait sûrement de bonnes intentions, mais en voulant former Louis et Othon à son image, il leur fit perdre le contact avec la réalité.

Quand Louis fêta son dix-huitième anniversaire et donc sa majorité, son père lui offrit une bourse remplie de pièces qui représentaient la monnaie valable dans toute la Bavière. N'ayant aucune expérience de l'argent, le jeune homme pensa qu'il pourrait acheter avec cette somme un médaillon précieux pour sa mère. Il fut amèrement déçu de voir qu'il n'en était rien. Après cette expérience, dit-on, Louis II ne s'est plus jamais préoccupé de la valeur de l'argent.

Toutefois, il s'est toujours trouvé des historiens pour imputer la destinée tragique des deux princes à l'hérédité, non à l'éducation. Selon eux, la dégénérescence proviendrait « du fait qu'un représentant de santé délicate de la dynastie des Wittelsbach a trouvé dans le sang de sa femme, alliage de Hohenzollern et de Brunswick, un complément des plus malheureux ». Finalement, c'est au duc Guillaume le Jeune de Brunswick, né en 1535, que Louis et Othon devraient leurs troubles mentaux.

La cause est donc entendue. Mais les amis et les admirateurs du roi Louis II de Bavière pensent (et ils ont leurs raisons), que leur roi de contes de fées, tout neurasthénique qu'il ait été, n'était certainement pas fou.

Der junge König

Berater hatten König Maximilian mehrfach nahegelegt, er möge sich bei seinen täglichen Spaziergängen im Englischen Garten wenigstens gelegentlich von seinem künftigen Nachfolger begleiten lassen. „Was soll ich mit ihm reden", antwortete die Majestät, der Sohn interessiere sich doch nicht für das, was man ihm sage. So blieb der Umgang der beiden Wittelsbacher weiterhin fast ausschließlich auf die kurzen, unergiebigen Begegnungen bei offiziellen Anlässen oder beim Frühstück und an der abendlichen Tafel beschränkt.

Aber auch die Mutter, eine Hohenzollern-Prinzessin, war offensichtlich nicht fähig, ein herzliches Verhältnis zu ihren beiden Söhnen zu finden. So kam es, daß Ludwig II. sie in späteren Jahren „die Gemahlin meines Vorgängers" oder „die Inhaberin des 3. Feldartillerie-Regiments" nannte.

Der eben volljährig gewordene Kronprinz Ludwig war auf das hohe Amt also noch nicht vorbereitet, als sein Vater im März 1864 nach einer nur dreitägigen Krankheit starb. Es ist überliefert, daß Ludwig erblaßte, als ihn ein Diener erstmals mit „Majestät" anredete.

Von Anfang an hat er die Sympathie seiner Untertanen gewonnen. „Als er den Thron bestieg", schrieb sein Biograph Gottfried von Boehm, „erschien er vielen als ein Götterjüngling. Ein Apoll von Gestalt, schmückten ihn scheinbar alle Vorzüge des Geistes und Gemütes. Nicht nur die Frauenwelt schwärmte für ihn, auch ernste Männer empfanden den Zauber seiner angeborenen, vornehmen Liebenswürdigkeit."

Die Zuneigung seiner Minister gewann er sich in den ersten Monaten seiner Regierung durch den kindli-

The young king

King Maximilian's advisers had often suggested to him that on his daily walks in the English Garden he might like – at least sometimes – to be accompanied by his future successor. "But what am I supposed to say to him?" His Majesty answered; "after all, my son takes no interest in what other people tell him." And so contact between the two Wittelsbach royals continued to be restricted almost exclusively to brief arid encounters at official occasions or over breakfast or the evening meal. But evidently the mother too, a Hohenzollern princess, was incapable of forming a warm relationship with her two sons, with the result that in later years Ludwig II referred to her as "my predecessor's consort" or "the colonel-in-chief of the 3rd Field Artillery Regiment"! Thus it was that Crown Prince Ludwig, who had just come of age, was not prepared for high office when in March 1864 his father died after a three-day illness. A report has come down to us that Ludwig turned pale when a servant addressed him for the first time as "Your Majesty".

Right from the beginning the new king won the affection of his subjects. "When Ludwig came to the throne," his biographer Gottfried von Boehm wrote, "he appeared to many like a veritable young god. This Apollo-like figure was seemingly blessed with all the mental and spiritual qualities that Nature can bestow upon a person. He was adored not only by women. Men too were touched by his innate nobility, kindliness and charm."

In the first months of his reign, he gained the affection of his ministers through the childlike enthusi-

Der junge König in Generaluniform mit Krönungsmantel, gemalt von Karl Piloty 1865.

The young king in general's uniform with coronation cloak, painted by Karl Piloty in 1865.

Le jeune roi en uniforme de général et portant le manteau du sacre, peint par Karl Piloty en 1865.

LUDOVICUS II
BAVARIAE REX
MDCCCLXV

Kurz nach der Thronbesteigung im Jahre 1864 malte Wilhelm Tauber den König in Offiziersuniform.

Shortly after Ludwig's accession to the throne in 1864, Wilhelm Tauber painted the king in officer's uniform.

Le roi en uniforme d'officier peint par Wilhelm Tauber peu de temps après son avènement en 1864.

Seite 14–15: Schloß Hohenschwangau mit Alp- und Schwansee.

Page 14–15: Hohenschwangau Castle with Lakes Alp and Schwan.

Pages 14–15 : Le château Hohenschwangau avec les lacs Alpsee et Schwansee.

Le jeune roi

Les conseillers de Maximilien II lui avaient suggéré à plusieurs reprises de se faire accompagner, au moins de temps en temps, par son futur successeur au cours de ses promenades quotidiennes dans le Jardin anglais. Le roi répondait invariablement qu'il ne savait pas de quoi lui parler, que de toute façon son fils ne s'intéressait pas à ce qu'on lui disait. Ainsi les relations entre les deux Wittelsbach restèrent presque exclusivement limitées aux brèves et stériles rencontres officielles ou au petit déjeuner et au dîner.

Même leur mère, une princesse Hohenzollern, ne fut manifestement pas capable de se faire aimer de ses deux fils, et plus tard, Louis II l'appellera, « l'épouse de mon prédécesseur » ou « la propriétaire du troisième régiment d'artillerie ».

Le kronprinz Louis était à peine majeur quand son père mourut en mars 1864 après trois jours de maladie. Le jeune homme n'était pas préparé à ses fonctions, on raconte qu'il aurait pâli quand un serviteur le nomma Majesté pour la première fois.

Dès le départ, ses sujets l'aimèrent. « Quand il monta sur le trône » écrivit son biographe Gottfried von Boehm, « il apparut à beaucoup comme un jeune dieu. Un Apollon de par sa silhouette, pourvu de tous les dons de l'esprit et du cœur. Les femmes n'étaient pas les seules à raffoler de lui, des hommes sérieux aussi étaient sensibles au charme de son amabilité naturelle distinguée. »

Il gagna la sympathie de ses ministres au cours des premiers mois de son règne par le zèle enfantin avec lequel il étudiait les dossiers qu'on lui soumettait. Il arrivait aussi sans cesse qu'il fit demander impatiemment s'il n'y avait rien de nouveau à lire ou à signer.

Son père avait demandé un jour à un érudit si la science pouvait fournir la preuve que les souverains avaient encore droit dans l'au-delà à une position privilégiée. La monarchie occupa bientôt aussi pour Louis II une place prépondérante. A cette époque, les peuples de l'Europe se battaient pour leurs droits et leurs libertés – l'aïeul du roi de Bavière avait d'ailleurs perdu son trône au cours de ces combats – cela n'empêchait pas Louis II

Nur auf diesem 1867/68 von Conrad Hoff
gemalten Aquarell ist das Audienzzimmer in
der Münchner Residenz zu sehen.

Today the audience room in the Munich residence survives only in this watercolour, painted
by Conrad Hoff in 1867–68.

La salle d'audience de la résidence de Munich
n'existe plus que dans cette aquarelle de Conrad
Hoff peinte en 1867/68.

Hoheiten anno 1864 in Bad Kissingen; König
Ludwig mit Kaiserin Elisabeth und dem russi-
schen Zarenpaar.

Royal company in Bad Kissingen in 1864:
King Ludwig with the Empress Elisabeth and
the Russian Tsar and Tsarina.

Les Altesses en 1864 à Bad Kissingen: Louis II
avec l'impératrice Elisabeth et le tsar et la tsarine russes.

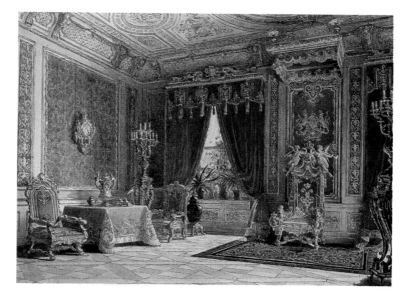

Zu den ersten Bauaufträgen seiner zweiundzwanzigjährigen Regierungszeit – und den ganz wenigen Projekten, die er in München realisierte – gehörte der Bau eines Wintergartens auf dem Nordflügel der Residenz.

Obwohl sich über diesem Wintergarten, den König Ludwig II. von seinem Arbeitszimmer aus betreten konnte, eine nach der damals modernsten Technik gestaltete Glas-Stahlkonstruktion wölbte, war die Gartenanlage selbst ein bizarres Nebeneinander der Stile.

Neben einer Tropfsteingrotte gab es einen maurischen Kiosk, ein indisches Königszelt, eine indische Fischerhütte, einen künstlich illuminierten Regenbogen und wechselndes Mondlicht. Hinzu kam, inmitten der vom Hofgärtner Effner arrangierten tropischen Vegetation, ein kleiner See mit einem Fischerboot.

Nach dem Tode des Königs gab es für den Wintergarten keine Verwendung mehr, und so wurde er 1897 abgerissen. Der Hofgartentrakt der Residenz, auf deren westlichem Teil er errichtet war (auf dem Bild der rechte Teil des Baus) zeigte sich damit wieder so, wie er früher ausgesehen hat.

One of Ludwig's first architectural commissions in his twenty-two-year reign – and one of the very few projects that he realized in Munich – was the construction of a winter garden on top of the north wing of the residence.

This rooftop garden, which King Ludwig II could access by stepping out of his study, was overarched by a technical advanced steel and glass construction. The garden itself was a bizarre juxtaposition of styles.

Besides a dripstone grotto there was a Moorish kiosk or pavilion, an Indian royal tent, an Indian fishing hut, an artificially illuminated rainbow, and intermittent moonlight. And as if that were not enough, there was also a small lake with a fishing boat surrounded by tropical vegetation laid out by Effner, the court gardener.

After the king's death, no one had any further use for the winter garden, and in 1897 it was demolished. The residence's Hofgarten or court garden wing, on which the winter garden had been built (the right part of the building in the illustration), then reverted to its original appearance.

Le jardin d'hiver que Louis II fit construire dans l'aile nord de la résidence est l'une de ses premières commandes et l'un des rares projets réalisés à Munich au cours de ses vingt-deux ans de règne.

Si le dôme de verre et d'acier recouvrant le jardin d'hiver – Louis II pouvait l'atteindre de son bureau – est construit selon la technique la plus moderne de l'époque, le jardin lui-même est un mélange bizarre des styles les plus divers.

On y trouvait une grotte, un kiosque maure, une tente royale indienne, une cabane de pêcheurs indienne, un arc-en-ciel éclairé de manière artificielle et un clair de lune à la lumière changeante. S'y ajoutait, au milieu de la végétation tropicale agencée par le jardinier royal Effner, un petit lac avec une barque de pêcheurs.

Le roi disparu, le jardin d'hiver ne fut plus utilisé, et on le démolit en 1897. On peut ainsi contempler dans son état initial l'aile où se trouvait la cour-jardin de la résidence, sur la partie ouest de laquelle il était édifié (sur l'illustration, la partie droite du bâtiment).

Ein im Jahre 1874 gefertigtes Ordenskreuz des
St. Georg-Ritterordens. Es ist geschmückt mit
Rubinen, Brillanten und Smaragden.

A cross of the Order of the Knights of St George,
made in 1874 and adorned with rubies, dia-
monds and emeralds.

Une croix de l'ordre des Chevaliers de Saint-
Georges réalisée en 1874. Elle est ornée de
rubis, de diamants et d'émeraudes.

Als Großmeister des Hausritterordens vom Hl.
Georg erteilte König Ludwig am 26. April
1880 in der Alten Hofkapelle zum erstenmal
den Ritterschlag.

King Ludwig conferred his first knighthood as
Grand Master of the Royal Order of St George
on 26 April 1880 in the Old Royal Chapel.

Grand Maître de l'ordre des Chevaliers de
Saint-Georges, le roi arme un chevalier pour la
première fois dans l'ancienne chapelle de la
Cour, le 26 avril 1880.

Mit ordensgeschmückter Brust: Seine Majestät
König Ludwig II., kolorierter Lichtdruck,
um 1870.

A much-decorated and beribboned King Ludwig II, colour dye transfer print, c. 1870.

Sa Majesté le roi Louis II, la poitrine couverte
de décorations, héliogravure coloriée (à la
main), vers 1870.

Seite 19: Als König von Bayern war Ludwig II.
Großmeister des 1729 gegründeten Hausritterordens vom Hl. Georg.

Page 19: As the King of Bavaria, Ludwig II
was a Grand Master of the Royal Order of the
Knights of Saint George, founded in 1729.

Page 19: Le roi de Bavière était aussi Grand
Maître de l'ordre des Chevaliers de Saint-
Georges fondé en 1729.

chen Eifer, mit dem er die vorgelegten Akten studierte. Immer wieder kam es auch vor, daß er ungeduldig nachfragen ließ, ob es denn keine neuen Dokumente zu lesen oder zu unterschreiben gebe.

Schon sein Vater hatte einmal einen Gelehrten gefragt, ob die Wissenschaft einen festen Beweis liefern könne, daß den Herrschern auch im Jenseits eine Ausnahmestellung zugewiesen werde. Eine herausragende Stellung nahm das Königtum bald auch für seinen Sohn ein. In Europa stritten die Völker um Rechte und Freiheiten, der König von Bayern aber, dessen Großvater in diesen Kämpfen seine Krone verloren hatte, suchte sich seine Vorbilder in einer längst vergangenen, absolutistischen Zeit, bei Frankreichs Bourbonenkönigen.

Der Bayernkönig huldigte den verblichenen Majestäten – Ludwig XV. und seinen Damen in Linderhof, Ludwig XIV. auf Herrenchiemsee – und zelebrierte seine Regentschaft wie ein religiöses Ritual. So gleicht etwa der Thronsaal von Schloß Neuschwanstein sehr viel mehr dem Inneren einer Kirche als dem Repräsentationsraum eines weltlichen Herrschers.

Das höfische Zeremoniell bedeutete ihm mehr als das politische Geschäft. Er empfing in seinen frühen Jahren zwar Herrscher anderer Länder – zum Beispiel Kaiser Franz Joseph und Kaiserin Elisabeth in Bad Kissingen, die Zarin Maria Alexandrowna am Starnberger See, Kaiser Napoleon III. und Kaiserin Eugenie im Zug zwischen Augsburg und Prien am Chiemsee sowie den preußischen König Wilhelm in Hohenschwangau –, doch besucht hat er von seinen gekrönten Kollegen nur den französischen Kaiser, den er kurz vor der Begegnung in Augsburg bei der ersten seiner drei (sehr kurzen) Frankreichreisen traf. Nie war der Wittelsbacher dagegen in Wien oder Berlin gewesen, und selbst in seinem eigenen Lande ist er nur äußerst selten gereist.

Seine Wege führten meist bergwärts, dabei kam er freilich auch in die Schweiz, in die Heimat von Wilhelm Tell. Er mußte nicht reisen, um die Welt zu erfahren – er schuf sie sich in seiner Phantasie, er träumte sich die Wirklichkeit. Ludwig II. von Bayern war fürwahr, was der französische Dichter Paul Verlaine schrieb: der einzige wahre König des Jahrhunderts, „le seul vrai roi de ce siècle".

asm with which he studied documents submitted to him. Over and over again it happened that he impatiently enquired as to whether there were no new papers for him to read or sign.

His father had once asked a scholar whether science could provide copper-bottomed proof that rulers were also allocated a special position in the next kingdom. For his son, the Wittelsbach kingdom soon occupied an exceptional position here on earth. Whereas in much of Europe nations were struggling for rights and freedom, the King of Bavaria, whose grandfather had lost his crown in these upheavals, sought his models in long-forgotten absolutist times – with France's Bourbon kings. The Bavarian king paid homage to faded majesties – at Linderhof to Louis XV and his ladies, at Herrenchiemsee to Louis XIV – whose reign he celebrated like a religious ritual. Thus, for example, the throne room at Neuschwanstein Castle looks more like the inside of a church than the audience chamber of a worldly sovereign.

Courtly ceremonial meant more to Ludwig II than the business of politics. True, in his early years he received rulers from other countries – for example the Emperor Franz Joseph and his Empress Elisabeth in Bad Kissingen, Tsarina Maria Alexandrovna at Lake Starnberg, Emperor Napoleon III and the Empress Eugénie en route between Augsburg and Prien on the Chiemsee, and the Prussian King Wilhelm in Hohenschwangau – and yet the only one of his crowned colleagues whom he went out of his way to visit was the French emperor, whom he met shortly before the Augsburg encounter on the first of his three very brief trips to France. The Wittelsbach sovereign never once went to Vienna or Berlin, and even in his own country he travelled only extremely rarely. Most of his journeys took him "uphill", where he came of course to Switzerland, the land of William Tell. But he did not need to travel to discover the world – he created it in his imagination. He dreamed up reality. Ludwig II of Bavaria was indeed, as the French poet Paul Verlaine wrote, "le seul vrai roi de ce siècle" – this century's only real king.

de chercher ses modèles dans un monde depuis long-temps disparu, la monarchie absolue de l'Ancien Régime en France.

Louis II rendait hommage aux majestés défuntes – Louis XV et ses dames au château de Linderhof, Louis XIV à Herrenchiemsee – et célébrait son règne comme un rituel religieux. Rien d'étonnant donc si la salle du trône du château de Neuschwanstein évoque davantage l'intérieur d'une église que la salle d'apparat d'un souverain de ce monde.

Il accordait plus d'importance aux cérémonies officielles qu'aux affaires publiques, et s'il reçut dans ses premières années nombre de têtes couronnées – par exemple l'empereur François-Joseph et l'impératrice Elisabeth à Bad Kissingen, la tsarine Maria Alexandrovna au lac de Starnberg, l'empereur Napoléon III et l'impératrice Eugénie dans le train entre Augsbourg et Prien sur le Chiemsee ainsi que le roi prussien Guillaume à Hohenschwangau, il ne rendit visite pour sa part qu'à l'Empereur français, vu brièvement lors de la première de ses trois (très courtes) visites à Paris avant la rencontre d'Augsbourg. Jamais en revanche le roi de Bavière ne se rendra à Berlin ou Vienne, et même dans son propre pays, il ne se déplacera qu'extrêmement rarement.

Son chemin le menait le plus souvent dans les montagnes, et il arriva ainsi en Suisse, la patrie de Guillaume Tell. Il n'avait nul besoin de voyager pour faire l'expérience du monde – il le créait dans son imagination, il rêvait sa réalité. En vérité, pour reprendre les termes du poète français Paul Verlaine, Louis II de Bavière fut: « Le seul vrai roi de ce siècle ».

Während König Ludwig um 1869/70 der Bildhauerin Elisabeth Ney in einem der Hofgartenzimmer für diese Büste Modell saß, mußte ihm sein Kabinettchef aus Goethes „Iphigenie" vorlesen.

When King Ludwig sat for the sculptress Elisabeth Ney in one of the Hofgarten (court garden) rooms around 1869–70, his cabinet secretary was obliged to read to him from Goethe's "Iphigenie".

Louis II pose pour le sculpteur Elisabeth Ney dans le jardin d'hiver du palais en 1869/70 en écoutant son chef de cabinet lui lire l'« Iphigénie » de Goethe.

Im Mai 1864, nach ihrer ersten Begegnung, schrieb König Ludwig an Richard Wagner: „Seien Sie überzeugt, ich will alles tun, was irgend in meinen Kräften steht, um Sie für vergangene Leiden zu entschädigen."

In May 1864, following their first meeting, King Ludwig wrote to Richard Wagner: "Rest assured, I shall do everything in my power to have you recompensed for your past sufferings."

En mai 1864, après leur première rencontre, Louis II écrit à Richard Wagner « Soyez convaincu que je ferai tout ce qui est en mon pouvoir pour vous consoler de vos souffrances passées. »

Die Freundschaft mit Richard Wagner

Der wittelsbachische König Ludwig II. herrschte seit vier Wochen in Bayern, als er im April 1864 seinen Kabinettssekretär Franz von Pfistermeister mit einem Ring und einem königlichen Handschreiben ausschickte, Richard Wagner zu finden und nach München zu bringen. Am Ende einer kleinen Irrfahrt durch Österreich und Süddeutschland fand der Hofbeamte den von Gläubigern bedrängten Komponisten in Stuttgart. Am 5. Mai 1864 trat der 51jährige Wagner in der Münchner Residenz erstmals dem 18jährigen Bayernkönig gegenüber, der ihn mit seinen 1,91 Metern um mehr als Haupteslänge überragte.

An diesem Tag begann eine ungleiche, doch für den Komponisten finanziell wie künstlerisch ertragreiche Freundschaft. Unter dem Eindruck dieser so schicksalshaften Begegnung schrieb Wagner einer Freundin: „Er ist leider so schön und geistvoll, seelenvoll und herrlich, daß ich fürchte, sein Leben müsse wie ein flüchtiger Göttertraum in dieser gemeinen Welt zerrinnen."

Zu den huldigenden königlichen Worten kam auch noch viel königliches Geld: bereits am 9. Mai 1864 ein erstes Geschenk von 4000 Gulden (was dem Jahresgehalt eines Ministerialrates entsprach), dann noch ein Jahresgehalt von weiteren 4000 Gulden, im Juni ein Geschenk von 16 000 Gulden... Der König gab, der Meister nahm, und die Münchner schüttelten zunächst die Köpfe, begannen dann aber vernehmlich zu murren.

Sie hatten dazu erneut Anlaß, als bekannt wurde, daß ihr König seinem Favoriten über der Isar auch noch ein eigenes Opernhaus bauen wollte. Noch ehe das schicksalhafte Jahr 1864 zu Ende ging, kam der Architekt Gottfried Semper mit dem Modell des Hauses angereist. Es gab dann freilich Verzögerungen, mehrfach wurde der vorgesehene Bauplatz gewechselt und zuletzt wurde das ganze Projekt abgesagt.

Vielleicht trug dieses Scheitern die Schuld daran, daß sich König Ludwig II. in München als Bauherr kaum betätigte und den Aufenthalt in dieser Stadt, wann immer ihm dies möglich war, mied.

Begonnen hatte die Schwärmerei für Wagner 1861, als der 15-jährige Kronprinz Ludwig in der Hofoper eine

Friendship with Richard Wagner

In April 1864, four weeks after his coronation, the young King Ludwig II dispatched his cabinet secretary Franz von Pfistermeister with a ring and a royal handwritten letter to find Richard Wagner and bring him to Munich. After a small detour through Austria and southern Germany, the court official finally discovered the composer beleaguered by creditors in Stuttgart. On 5 May 1864, in the royal residence in Munich, the 51-year-old Wagner stood facing the 18-year-old Bavarian king for the first time. Ludwig, fully 1.91 metres tall (6 feet 10 inches), towered head and shoulders over the musician.

That day marked the beginning of a most unequal, but for the composer both financially and artistically highly advantageous friendship. Under the sway of their fateful meeting, Wagner wrote to a female friend: "Alas, he is so handsome and wise, soulful and lovely, that I fear that his life must melt away in this vulgar world like a fleeting dream of the gods."

The king's adulatory words were backed up by kingsize subventions. On 9 May 1864, only four days after their first meeting, an initial present of 4,000 florins (equivalent to a ministerial assistant's annual salary) winged its way to Wagner, then another annual emolument of a further 4,000 florins, and in June a gift of 16,000 florins... The king gave, the maestro took, and the good people of Munich at first shook their heads and then began to grumble audibly.

Bavaria's citizens had fresh reason to complain when it became known that their king, not content with this beneficence, also wanted to build his new-found favourite a personal opera house overlooking the River Isar. Before the fateful year 1864 was out, the architect Gottfried Semper arrived on the scene with a model of the house. Then, of course, there were delays, the intended construction site was repeatedly changed, and finally the whole project was dropped. Ludwig's mania for Wagner had begun in 1861, when the fifteen-year-old crown prince attended a performance of "Lohengrin" in the court opera. From that evening on he fell under the spell of both the music and the world of Wagner's operas (although his piano tutor – and later Wagner

Amitié et mécénat

En avril 1864, un mois après son couronnement, Louis II envoya son secrétaire de cabinet Franz von Pfistermeister, muni d'une missive de sa main et d'une bague, chercher Richard Wagner pour l'amener à Munich. Au terme d'un périple à travers l'Autriche et l'Allemagne du Sud, le fonctionnaire royal trouva le compositeur à Stuttgart, harcelé par ses créanciers. Le 5 mai 1864, Richard Wagner, âgé de cinquante et un ans, rencontra pour la première fois dans sa résidence de Munich le roi de Bavière.

Ce jour marque le début d'une amitié très inégale, aussi féconde sur le plan financier qu'artistique pour le compositeur. Encore sous l'impression de cette rencontre fatidique, Wagner écrivit à une amie: « Il est hélas si beau et plein d'esprit, sensible et superbe, que je crains que sa vie doive se dissiper dans ce monde vil comme un fugitif rêve divin. »

Le roi ne s'en tenait pas aux hommages enflammés, il envoyait de l'argent, beaucoup d'argent. Le 9 mai 1864, déjà, un premier don de quatre mille florins (ce qui correspondait au salaire annuel d'un conseiller ministériel), puis en outre un salaire annuel de quatre mille florins, en juin un cadeau de seize mille florins... Si bien que les Munichois se mirent à gronder...

Leur mécontentement trouva un nouvel objet quand il fut de notoriété publique que leur roi voulait faire construire un opéra à son favori allemand. L'année 1864 n'était pas à son terme que l'architecte Gottfried Semper présentait déjà ses plans. Mais il y eut des retards, l'emplacement prévu fut modifié à plusieurs reprises et finalement on finit par renoncer au projet.

La ferveur romanesque de Louis II pour Wagner avait commencé en 1861, alors que prince héritier âgé de quinze ans, il assistait à une représentation de « Lohengrin » donnée à l'opéra de la Cour. A partir de ce jour, il fut sous l'empire de la musique et des mythes wagnériens (pourtant son professeur de piano et plus tard le compositeur lui-même affirmeront que le roi n'avait pas l'oreille musicale).

Wagner reçut d'énormes sommes d'argent, en été 1864 une villa sur le lac de Starnberg, plus tard une villa à Munich. En juin 1865, il offrit en retour au roi ce qui

Mit „Thränen himmlischer Rührung" hatte sich Richard Wagner beim König für die Einladung nach München bedankt.

Richard Wagner had thanked the king for the royal invitation to Munich with "tears of heavenly emotion".

C'est avec des « larmes de divin émoi » que Richard Wagner avait remercié le roi pour son invitation à Munich.

In einer Brieftasche aus blauem Seidensamt verwahrte der König die Briefe seines Freundes Richard Wagner.

The king kept his letters from his friend Richard Wagner in a blue silk and velvet wallet.

Le roi conservait les lettres de son ami Richard Wagner dans un portefeuille en velours de soie bleu.

Für die Uraufführung von Wagners „Tristan und Isolde" am 10. Juni 1865 im Münchner Hof- und Nationaltheater schuf Angelo II. Quaglio dieses Bühnenmodell für den ersten Aufzug.

Angelo II Quaglio designed this stage set for the first act of Wagner's "Tristan and Isolde", premiered on 10 June 1865 in the Munich National Court Theatre.

Ces décors du premier acte de « Tristan et Isolde » sont signés Angelo II. Quaglio. La première eut lieu le 10 juin 1865 au Théâtre royal et national de Munich.

Für die Räume des Schlosses Neuschwanstein stellte König Ludwig ein Bildprogramm auf: „Tannhäuser" für das Arbeitszimmer, „Tristan und Isolde" für das Schlafzimmer, den „Ring des Nibelungen" in der Vorhalle.

Sein Wohnzimmer hat der König dem Andenken an Lohengrin gewidmet. Während Ferdinand von Piloty einen Schrank mit Bildern mittelalterlicher Dichter bemalte, sind auf den Gemälden an den Wänden Szenen aus der Lohengrin-Sage dargestellt. So zeigt Wilhelm Hauschild das „Gralswunder" mit der Erwählung des Ritters zum Streiter für Elsa. An der Nordseite malte August von Heckel (hier im Ausschnitt) die Ankunft Lohengrins. Der König hatte dem Künstler seine genauen Vorstellungen übermitteln lassen: „S. M. wünscht, daß die Kopfhaltung Lohengrins nicht zu schief ist."

King Ludwig selected pictorial themes for the rooms of Neuschwanstein Castle: "Tannhäuser" for his study, "Tristan and Isolde" for his bedroom, and the "Ring of the Nibelung" in the vestibule.

The king dedicated his living room to the memory of Lohengrin. A cupboard was covered with pictures of mediaeval poets painted by Ferdinand von Piloty, while paintings on the walls depicted scenes from the Lohengrin myth. Thus Wilhelm Hauschild could be seen showing the "Miracle of the Grail" with the election of the knight as Elsa's champion. On the north side, August von Heckel painted Lohengrin's arrival (the illustration shows only a detail). The king had his exact wishes conveyed to the artist: "H. M. desires that Lohengrin should not hold his head too much at an angle."

Louis II élabora un programme pictural pour les pièces du château de Neuschwanstein : «Tannhäuser » pour le bureau, «Tristan et Iseult » pour la chambre, « L'Anneau des Nibelungen » pour le vestibule. Le roi honora le souvenir de Lohengrin dans la salle à manger. Tandis que Ferdinand von Piloty a peint une armoire avec des motifs de poètes du Moyen Age, des scènes tirées de la Saga de Lohengrin sont représentées sur les tableaux accrochés aux murs. C'est ainsi que Wilhelm Hauschild montre le « Miracle du Graal » où un chevalier est choisi pour défendre la Comtesse Elsa. Pour la face nord, August von Heckel (détail de la reproduction) peignit l'arrivée de Lohengrin. Le roi avait fait savoir à l'artiste ce qu'il souhaitait : «Sa Majesté désire que Lohengrin n'ait pas la tête trop penchée. »

Karlsruhe verzichtete auf die Uraufführung, in Wien gab man die Oper nach siebzig Proben als unspielbar zurück, schließlich gab König Ludwig 1865 seinem Freund Richard Wagner die Möglichkeit, „Tristan und Isolde" an seinem Hoftheater herauszubringen. Die Majestät war bereits nach der Generalprobe von dem Werk so beeindruckt, daß sie ihr auf dem Starnberger See verkehrendes Schiff „Maximilian" in „Tristan" umtaufte.

Daß die Uraufführung am 6. Juni 1865 zu einem großen Erfolg wurde, war vor allem auch dem Ehepaar Ludwig und Malvine Schnorr von Carolsfeld zu danken, das die Titelrollen sang.

Karlsruhe declined to stage the premiere of "Tristan and Isolde", Vienna returned the opera after seventy rehearsals as unplayable, and in the end it was left to King Ludwig to provide his friend Richard Wagner with an opportunity to give the work its first airing, allowing Wagner to use the Court Theatre. His Majesty was already so impressed by the opera at its dress-rehearsal stage that he changed the name of his boat on Lake Starnberg from "Maximilian" to "Tristan"!

The success of the premiere on 6 June 1865 was largely due to the married couple Ludwig and Malvine Schnorr from Carolsfeld, who sang the title roles.

Après que l'on eut renoncé à la première à Karlsruhe et qu'à Vienne on eut rendu l'opéra au bout de soixante-dix répétitions en décrétant qu'il n'était pas jouable, Louis II donna finalement en 1865 à son ami Wagner l'occasion de représenter «Tristan et Isolde» au Hoftheater. Après la répétition générale, Sa Majesté fut tellement impressionnée par l'œuvre qu'elle rebaptisa du nom de «Tristan» son bateau «Maximilien» qui circulait sur le lac de Starnberg.

Si la première, qui eut lieu le 6 juin 1865, connut un grand succès, ce fut aussi grâce au couple Ludwig et Malvine Schnorr von Carolsfeld qui chanta les rôles principaux.

Empfang in Wagners Villa Wahnfried anläßlich der zweiten Bayreuther Festspiele 1882. Von links nach rechts: Lenbach, Cosima Wagner mit Sohn Siegfried, mit einer Partitur (und dem berühmten Barett) der Meister, am Flügel Franz Liszt.

Reception in Wagner's villa "Wahnfried" at the time of the second Bayreuth festival in 1882. From left to right: Lenbach, Cosima Wagner with her son Siegfried, the maestro himself holding a score (and wearing his famous beret), and Franz Liszt at the piano.

Réception à la Villa Wahnfried de Wagner à l'occasion du second festival de Bayreuth en 1882. De gauche à droite : Lenbach, Cosima Wagner et son fils Siegfried, le maître avec une partition (et son fameux béret), et au piano Franz Liszt.

Wahrscheinlich nach photographischen Vorlagen schuf Franz von Lenbach das Bild des Königs als Großmeister des Hausritterordens vom Hl. Hubertus.

Franz von Lenbach probably based his painting of the king as Grand Master of the Royal Order of the Knights of St Hubertus on photographs.

Franz von Lenbach peignit probablement d'après des photographies ce portrait du roi en tant que Grand Maître des chevaliers de Saint-Hubert.

Aufführung des „Lohengrin" besuchte. Von diesem Abend an war er der Musik und der Welt der Wagner-Opern verfallen (obwohl sein Klavierlehrer und später auch Wagner behaupteten, der König sei unmusikalisch).

Wagner erhielt enorme Geldbeträge, im Sommer 1864 eine Villa am Starnberger See, später eine Villa in München. Doch im Juni 1865 erfolgte die angemessene Gegengabe, der vielleicht größte Tag in der Musikgeschichte der bayerischen Landeshauptstadt: die Uraufführung von „Tristan und Isolde".

Die Mittel flossen weiterhin reichlich, denn dem Meister sollte es möglich gemacht werden, die „Meistersinger" und den „Ring des Nibelungen" zu vollenden. Ehe es aber zur Uraufführung kam, mußte Wagner die Stadt verlassen. Daß ihr König den ehemaligen sächsischen Hofkapellmeister mit viel Geld bedachte, hätten die Münchner wohl hingenommen, doch als Wagner sich auch noch in die politischen Geschäfte einmischte, drängten sie die Majestät, den fürwahr teuren Freund ins Schweizer Exil von Tribschen zu schicken. An einem Dezembermorgen 1865 verließ der Komponist die Stadt. Die Liebe seines Königs (und dessen finanzielle Großzügigkeit) blieb ihm aber erhalten.

Er brauchte sie vor allem, als er in Bayreuth seinen Traum vom eigenen Festspielhaus verwirklichte. Etwa zwei Jahre nach der Grundsteinlegung ging das Geld aus, und da kein deutscher Fürst half – und Bismarck nicht einmal antwortete –, bewilligte König Ludwig II. im Frühjahr 1874 einen Kredit von 100 000 Talern. Als dann in Bayreuth am 13. August 1876 das Haus auf dem Grünen Hügel festlich eröffnet wurde, war der Bayernkönig nicht unter den Festgästen. Er hatte die Einladung abgelehnt – vielleicht weil er dem bei der Premiere anwesenden Kaiser Wilhelm nicht begegnen wollte – und war statt dessen eine Woche zuvor zur Generalprobe des „Ring" angereist.

Als Richard Wagner im Februar 1883 gestorben war, sagte Ludwig zu seinem Hofsekretär: „Den Künstler, um welchen jetzt die ganze Welt trauert, habe ich zuerst erkannt, habe ich der Welt gerettet." An seinem Münchner Hoftheater waren einst „Tristan und Isolde", die „Meistersänger von Nürnberg", „Rheingold" und (gegen den Willen Wagners) die „Walküre" uraufgeführt worden.

himself – maintained that the king had no ear for music).

Wagner received enormous sums of money, in the summer of 1864 a villa on Lake Starnberg, and later a villa in Munich. But in June 1865 he reciprocated with a commensurate return gift – perhaps the greatest day in the musical history of the Bavarian capital: the world premiere of "Tristan and Isolde". The funds continued to flow generously, enabling the maestro to complete the "Mastersingers" and the "Ring of the Nibelung". However, before the premieres of these operas had taken place, Wagner had to leave the city. The people of Munich might have accepted their king's extravagant generosity towards the one-time Saxon court director of music, but when Wagner started to get involved in politics, they urged His Majesty to send his inestimable friend, however worthy, into Swiss exile at Tribschen. One December morning in 1865 the composer left the capital with his servants and dog. But that was not the end of the king's adoration of the composer or his financial generosity towards the maestro.

Wagner needed this royal patronage above all when he came to realize his dream of a festival theatre of his own in Bayreuth. Some two years after the foundation stone had been laid, he ran out of money, and because no German ruler was willing to stump up – Bismarck did not even reply – King Ludwig II approved in spring 1874 a loan of 100,000 thalers. At the time he had enough bills of his own to pay: shortly before he had bought Herren Island on the Chiemsee, and at Linderhof work was making good progress. However, when the House on the Green Hill was ceremonially opened in Bayreuth on 13 August 1876, the Bavarian king was not among the festival guests. He had declined his invitation – perhaps because he did not want to run into Emperor Wilhelm on the opening night – and had travelled instead a week earlier to the dress rehearsal of the "Ring".

When Richard Wagner died in February 1883, the king said to his court secretary: "The artist whom the whole world now mourns was first recognized by me and saved from the world by me." "Tristan and Isolde", the "Mastersingers of Nuremberg", "Rhinegold" and (against Wagner's wishes) the "Valkyrie" all had their first performances at Ludwig's court theatre in Munich.

fut peut-être le plus grand jour dans l'histoire musicale de la capitale bavaroise: la première de « Tristan et Isolde ».

L'argent continuait de couler abondamment, car il fallait que le maître puisse achever les « Maîtres chanteurs » de Nuremberg et « L'Anneau du Nibelung ». Mais Wagner dut quitter la ville avant la première car les Munichois ne pouvaient accepter de le voir se mêler de politique et ils poussèrent le roi à envoyer son cher, trop cher ami en exil à Tribschen en Suisse. Par un matin de décembre 1865, le compositeur quitta la ville avec son chien et ses gens. Mais l'amitié du roi lui était assurée – et sa prodigalité ne tarit pas.

Wagner en eut grand besoin quand il réalisa à Bayreuth le rêve de sa vie, un théâtre. L'argent vint à manquer deux ans après la mise en chantier, et comme aucun prince allemand ne l'aidait, Louis II lui accorda au printemps 1874 un crédit de cent mille thalers. Pourtant, il avait à cette époque suffisamment de factures personnelles à régler, il venait en effet d'acquérir la Herreninsel sur le lac de Chiem, et les travaux avançaient rapidement au Linderhof.

Quand Richard Wagner mourut en février 1883, le roi dit à son secrétaire: « Cet artiste aujourd'hui pleuré par tous, c'est moi qui l'ai reconnu le premier, je l'ai sauvé pour le monde. » C'est dans son Hoftheater munichois qu'avaient été présentées les premières de Tristan et Isolde, « Les Maîtres chanteurs de Nuremberg », « L'Or du Rhin », et (contre la volonté de Wagner), « La Walkyrie ».

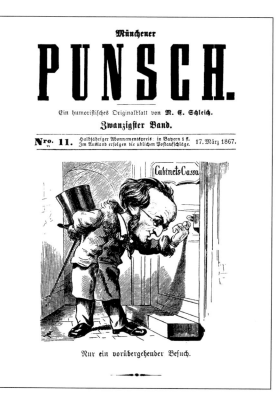

Ludwigs Vorgänger im königlichen Amt hatten sich für die Ausstattung der bayerischen Armee nicht sonderlich interessiert. Das Geld, meinten sie, sei besser angelegt, wenn damit große Bauten errichtet oder gelehrte „Nordlichter" berufen würden.

So übernahm Ludwig 1864 ein Heer, das schlecht trainiert, dürftig bewaffnet und somit nur bedingt einsatzbereit war, und diese Truppen mußte der Wittelsbacher 1866 zusammen mit den Österreichern in den Krieg gegen Preußen schicken.

Er selbst nahm an dieser ihm höchst widrigen Angelegenheit kaum Anteil. Während sich die feindlichen Parteien auf den Waffengang vorbereiteten, saß König Ludwig mit Freunden auf der Roseninsel im Starnberger See und mußte förmlich überredet werden, den Mobilmachungsbefehl zu unterzeichnen. Danach sprach er von Abdankung und meinte, man könne ja sagen, er sei geistig nicht ganz gesund.

Während die Truppen sich für den bevorstehenden Kampf rüsteten, stahl sich ihr Oberbefehlshaber in aller Heimlichkeit aus seinem Inselschlößchen fort und reiste – ohne irgend jemanden davon zu unterrichten und ohne für irgend jemanden erreichbar zu sein – in die Schweiz, nach Tribschen, um mit dem großzügig alimentierten Freund Richard Wagner dessen 53. Geburtstag zu feiern.

Ludwig II's royal predecessors had not interested themselves especially in equipping the Bavarian army. The money, they believed, was better invested in putting up prestigious buildings or in attracting erudite professorial luminaries from the north. Thus in 1864 Ludwig inherited an army that was badly trained, poorly armed, and hence only partly ready for action. And yet in 1866 it was these troops that the Wittelsbach ruler had to send together with the Austrians to war against Prussia.

He himself played almost no part in this, for him, highly repugnant affair. While the hostile parties were making preparations for the armed encounter, King Ludwig sat with friends on Rose Island in Lake Starnberg and literally had to be talked into signing the mobilization order. Afterwards he spoke of abdicating, adding that it could be put about that he was not in the best of mental health.

Whilst his troops were arming themselves for the impending clash, their commander-in-chief secretly stole away from his little island castle and travelled, to Tribschen in Switzerland. Here, safely out of reach, he celebrated the 53rd birthday of his lavishly maintained friend Richard Wagner. A few days later he was back again at Rose Island, had a firework display, and made a brief visit to army headquarters in Bamberg.

The war came – and was lost within just a few

Im deutschen Bruderkrieg von 1866 wurden die schlechtgerüsteten Bayern von den Preußen – wie in der Schlacht bei Üttingen – schnell geschlagen.

In the fratricidal German war of 1866 – as in the Battle of Üttingen – the poorly equipped Bavarians were quickly defeated by the Prussians.

Pendant la guerre des Etats allemands de 1866, les Prussiens eurent vite fait de défaire les Bavarois mal équipés, ici à la bataille d'Üttingen.

Les guerres de 1866 et 1870

Ceux qui avaient précédé le roi dans sa tâche ne s'étaient guère intéressés à l'équipement de l'armée bavaroise. Ils pensaient que l'argent était mieux placé s'il servait à construire de grands édifices ou à rémunérer les « lumières du Nord », les érudits mandés à la Cour. A son arrivée au pouvoir en 1864, Louis II trouva une armée mal entraînée, armée avec parcimonie et donc opérationnelle sous réserves, et il lui fallut l'envoyer combattre les Prussiens en 1866 aux côtés des troupes autrichiennes.

Lui-même prit à peine part à cette affaire qui le répugnait. Alors que les adversaires se préparaient à prendre les armes, le roi séjournait avec des amis à l'Ile des Roses sur le lac de Starnberg, et il fallut littéralement le convaincre de signer l'ordre de mobilisation. Il parla ensuite d'abdication, déclarant que l'on pourrait dire qu'il n'était pas tout à fait sain d'esprit.

Pendant que les troupes s'apprêtaient à affronter l'ennemi, leur commandant suprême se retira en cachette dans son petit château de l'Ile des Roses et s'en fut – sans prévenir qui que ce soit et impossible à joindre – en Suisse, à Tribschen, pour fêter les cinquante-trois ans de son ami Richard Wagner, généreusement pourvu par ses soins.

Quelques jours plus tard, de retour à l'Ile des Roses, il organisa des feux d'artifice avec ses amis et honora brièvement de sa présence le grand quartier général de Bamberg.

La guerre éclata – et fut perdue en l'espace de quelques jours. La Bavière dut payer trente millions de florins à la Prusse et signer un traité d'alliance secret avec les vainqueurs. Le roi parla de nouveau d'abdication, songea au suicide... et continua à régner.

Quatre ans plus tard, Bismarck qui voulait entrer en guerre demanda l'application du traité: l'armée bavaroise dut affronter la France aux côtés des troupes prussiennes et sous commandement supérieur prussien.

Pendant que les diplomates échangeaient des dépêches et que les grands quartiers généraux préparaient le déploiement des troupes, le roi de Bavière résidait loin de la capitale dans son palais de Linderhof

Obwohl an allem Militärischen desinteressiert, zeigte sich Ludwig II. in seinen frühen Regierungsjahren gerne in Uniform.

Although indifferent to all things military, in the early years of his reign Ludwig II liked to be seen in uniform.

Bien qu'indifférent aux affaires militaires, le roi Louis II semble apprécier l'uniforme dans les premières années de son règne.

Otto von Bismarck schätzte den Wittelsbacher, benutzte ihn für seine politischen Ziele und beschenkte ihn hinterher mit Geld aus dem Welfenfonds.

Otto von Bismarck valued the Wittelsbach monarch, used him to achieve his own political ends, and afterwards presented him with money from the Guelphic Fund.

Otto von Bismarck estimait Louis II, qu'il utilisa pour ses fins politiques avant de lui offrir de l'argent provenant du fonds des Guelfes.

Einige Tage später war er wieder zurück auf der Roseninsel, brannte mit seinen Freunden Feuerwerke ab und machte eine kurze Visite im Hauptquartier zu Bamberg.

Der Krieg kam – und ging innerhalb weniger Wochen verloren. Bayern mußte 30 Millionen Gulden an Preußen zahlen und einen geheimen Bündnisvertrag mit den Siegern unterzeichnen. Der König sprach wieder von Abdankung, dachte auch an Selbstmord ... und regierte weiter.

Vier Jahre nach der Niederlage im Deutschen Bruderkrieg wurde die Einlösung des Vertrages verlangt: Bayern mußte mit den preußischen Truppen und unter preußischem Oberbefehl gen Frankreich ziehen.

Während die Diplomaten Depeschen tauschten und die Generalstäbe den Aufmarsch vorbereiteten, residierte der bayerische König fernab der Hauptstadt in seinem Schloß Linderhof, „ohne alle Kenntnisse der augenblicklichen Weltlage". Das schrieb der Hofsekretär nach einem Besuch am 14. Juli 1870. Und einen Tag später erklärte Frankreich den Krieg.

Der König reiste nun nach Schloß Berg am Starnberger See, empfing morgens, noch im Bett, seinen Kabinettsekretär und gab den Mobilmachungsbefehl.

Napoleon III. wurde besiegt und Bismarck war am Ziel: der Beitritt der süddeutschen Staaten vollendete die Reichsbildung. König Ludwig II. hatte gehofft, man werde ihm, dessen Truppen sich im Kriege vielfach ausgezeichnet hatten, kleine Gebietserweiterungen zugestehen. Stattdessen mußte er, der Vertreter des ältesten deutschen Königsgeschlechtes, dem siegreichen Preußenkönig Wilhelm die deutsche Kaiserkrone antragen.

Der Bayer wußte, daß Berlin seinem Lande „die Euthanasie bereiten und es mit sanfter Hand zum Tode führen wollte" – so hatte der Hohenzollern-Gesandte in München in einem Brief geschrieben –, und um dazu nicht noch freiwillig und demonstrativ die Hand zu reichen, war Ludwig nicht nach Versailles gefahren.

Kommt der Prophet nicht zum Berg, so muß der Berg zum Propheten: Bismarck verfaßte den Brief, den er sich vom Bayernkönig wünschte, und schickte einen Boten damit nach Hohenschwangau, wo sich – unter starken Zahnschmerzen leidend – die Majestät aufhielt. Der Brief, in dem der Wittelsbacher im Namen der deutschen Fürsten dem Hohenzollern die Kaiserkrone

weeks. Bavaria had to pay 30 million florins to Prussia and sign a secret pact of alliance with the victors. The king again spoke of abdicating, even contemplated suicide – but continued ruling.

Four years after this defeat in the fratricidal German war, Prussia called for the pact to be redeemed: Bavaria had to march with Prussian troops and under Prussian command against France. While the diplomats exchanged dispatches and the general staffs prepared for deployment, the Bavarian king resided far away from the capital in Linderhof, one of his castles, "quite ignorant of the present international situation", as his court secretary wrote after a visit on 14 July 1870. And a day later France declared war.

Hearing this, the king travelled to Berg Castle on Lake Starnberg, received – still in bed – his cabinet secretary, and gave the order to mobilize. Napoleon III was defeated, and Bismarck had achieved his objective: to complete the formation of a Reich through the accession of the south-German states. King Ludwig II had hoped that, as a result of his troops having distinguished themselves so multifariously in the war, he would be granted small territorial expansions. Instead, he, the representative of the oldest German royal lineage, had to offer the victorious Prussian King Wilhelm the German imperial crown.

The Bavarian knew that Berlin was "preparing euthanasia [for his country], wanting to dispatch it with a velvet-gloved hand" – thus the Hohenzollern envoy in Munich wrote in a letter – and in order not to seem to willingly invite the coup de grace himself, Ludwig had deliberately not gone to Versailles. If the mountain won't come to Mohammed, then Mohammed must go to the mountain – Bismarck drew up the letter he want-

« sans avoir toute connaissance de la situation du monde à cet instant », ainsi que l'écrivit le secrétaire de la Cour après lui avoir rendu visite le 14 juillet 1870. Le lendemain, la France déclarait la guerre.

Le roi se rendit alors au château de Berg sur les rives du lac de Starnberg, reçut le matin encore couché son secrétaire de cabinet et signa l'ordre de mobilisation. Napoléon III vaincu, Bismarck avait atteint son but: l'entrée des quatre Etats du Sud dans la confédération germanique parachevait l'unité allemande. Louis II avait espéré, lui dont les troupes s'étaient distinguées de si multiples façons, qu'on lui concéderait un petit élargissement de son territoire. Au lieu de cela, le représentant de la plus ancienne dynastie royale allemande dut offrir la couronne impériale allemande au roi de Prusse, Guillaume.

Le roi de Bavière savait que Berlin « voulait préparer l'euthanasie » à son pays « et le conduire d'une main douce à la mort », c'est ce qu'écrit dans une lettre de Munich l'envoyé des Hohenzollern – et pour ne pas en outre y prêter la main de manière volontaire et démonstrative, Louis II avait refusé d'assister aux cérémonies se

anträgt, wurde geschrieben und so konnte am 18. Januar 1871 im Spiegelsaal von Versailles das Zweite Deutsche Reich ausgerufen werden. Bayern aber hatte damit einen Gutteil seiner Souveränität verloren.

Ludwig II. dachte wieder an Abdankung, doch sein Bruder Otto war bereits zu krank, um ihm nachzufolgen.

ed from the Bavarian king and sent a messenger with it to Hohenschwangau, where His Majesty, suffering from bad toothache, was staying. The letter, in which the Wittelsbach monarch offered the imperial crown to the Hohenzollern on behalf of the German rulers, was signed, thus enabling the Second German Reich to be proclaimed on 18 January 1871 in the Hall of Mirrors at Versailles, and entailing for Bavaria the loss of a large part of its sovereignty. Ludwig's thoughts turned once more to abdication, but his brother Otto was already too ill to succeed him.

déroulant à Versailles. Peine perdue… la montagne vint à lui…: Bismarck rédigea un modèle de la lettre qu'il désirait recevoir du roi de Bavière et la lui fit porter par un messager à Hohenschwangau où Louis II séjournait, souffrant d'une terrible rage de dents. La lettre dans laquelle Louis de Wittelsbach, au nom de tous les princes allemands, offre la couronne impériale à Guillaume de Hohenzollern fut écrite, et c'est ainsi que le 18 janvier 1871, le second Reich put être proclamé dans la Galerie des Glaces de Versailles. La Bavière, devenue l'un des vingt-cinq Etats de l'empire allemand, perdait une grande partie de son autonomie.

De nouveau, Louis II pensa abdiquer, mais son frère Othon était déjà trop atteint pour prendre sa suite.

König Ludwig nahm am 16. Juni 1871 die Parade ab, als die siegreichen bayerischen Truppen unter Führung des preußischen Kronprinzen Friedrich Wilhelm in München einzogen.

On 16 June 1871 King Ludwig took the salute, when the victorious Bavarian troops marched into Munich under the command of the Prussian crown prince Friedrich Wilhelm.

Louis II à la parade le 16 juin 1871, quand les troupes bavaroises victorieuses sous le commandement du kronprinz prussien Frédéric-Guillaume entrent à Munich.

Seite 38: Ein bayerischer Chevauleger rettet im Deutsch-Französischen Krieg einen gestürzten preußischen Husaren vor seinen Verfolgern.

Page 38: A Bavarian light cavalryman rescues a fallen Prussian hussar from his pursuers in the Franco-Prussian War of 1870.

Page 38: Un chevau-léger bavarois sauvant un hussard prussien tombé de cheval pendant la guerre franco-allemande de 1870.

Die Verlobung mit Sophie

Engagement to Sophie

Es war alles ein wenig überstürzt und sicher auch un-überlegt. Der junge König hatte an jenem Januartag des Jahres 1867 einen Ball besucht, war erst am frühen Morgen in die Residenz zurückgekommen, und statt ins Bett zu gehen, ließ er sich um 6 Uhr bei seiner Mutter melden, die er darum bat, für ihn bei seinem Großonkel Max, dem Herzog in Bayern, um die Hand seiner Tochter Sophie anzuhalten. Eine Stunde später war die Verlobung beschlossen und um 9 Uhr vormittags wurde sie der Öffentlichkeit bekanntgemacht: König Ludwig II. von Bayern hat sich am 22. Januar mit Sophie, Herzogin in Bayern und Schwester der österreichischen Kaiserin Elisabeth, verlobt.

Am Geburtstag des Monarchen, am 25. August, sollte die Hochzeit sein. Ein Brautmarsch wurde komponiert, Gedenkmünzen geprägt und eine Hochzeitskarosse im Wert von einer Million Gulden in Auftrag gegeben – doch der 25. August verstrich, und noch einige weitere Termine vergingen, bis schließlich am 7. Oktober auf Wunsch des Brautvaters der Bund gelöst wurde, noch ehe er geschlossen war.

Einige Tage vor der Verlobung hatte Sophie einen Brief des Königs erhalten und dabei erfahren, was sie ohnedies wußte: „Der Hauptinhalt unseres Verkehrs war stets... Richard Wagners merkwürdiges, ergreifendes Geschick". Als dann das Schlußwort gesprochen war, erhielt sie diese Nachricht: „Geliebte Elsa! Dein grausamer Vater reißt uns auseinander. Ewig Dein Heinrich." Welch ein Brautpaar und welch eine Verbindung, wo der Bräutigam für sich und seine künftige Frau die Namen wagnerscher Opernfiguren wählt!

Die herzogliche Prinzessin wird unter der Trennung dieser seltsamen Liaison nicht allzusehr gelitten haben, denn in der Verlobungszeit erlebte sie eine kurze Romanze mit dem feschen Photographen Edgar Hanf-staengl. Drei Tage nach ihrer Verlobung ist ihm Sophie erstmals begegnet, und während der Bräutigam im Juli 1867 unter dem Pseudonym „Graf von Berg" die Weltausstellung in Paris besuchte, turtelte daheim in Bayern das Fräulein Braut mit ihrem „theueren, liebsten Freund", dem sie in einem Brief klagte: „Warum mußte

It all came about somewhat precipitately, indeed rashly. One January day in 1867 the young king had gone to a ball, not returning to his residence until the early hours of the next day. Instead of going to bed, he had had himself announced at 6 o'clock to his mother and persuaded her to ask his great-uncle Max, the Duke of Bavaria, for the hand of the duke's daughter Sophie in marriage. An hour later the engagement was concluded and at 9 o'clock in the morning announced to the public: King Ludwig II of Bavaria has become engaged on 22 January to Sophie, Duchess of Bavaria and sister of the Austrian Empress Elisabeth. The wedding was set for 25 August, the monarch's birthday. A nuptial march was composed, commemorative coins struck, and a wedding coach commissioned at a cost of one million florins – but 25 August came and went, as did several other proposed dates, until finally on 7 October, at the request of the bride's father, the union was dissolved even before it had been solemnized.

A few days before the engagement Sophie had received a letter from the king telling her what she already knew: "The main substance of our relationship has always been ... Richard Wagner's remarkable and deeply moving destiny." And when a curtain had been drawn on the matter, she received this message: "My beloved Elsa! Your cruel father has torn us apart. Eternally yours, Heinrich." What a betrothal, where the groom chooses the names of Wagnerian opera figures for himself and his bride! But the ducal princess cannot have suffered overmuch from the break-up of this singular liaison, for during the engagement period she had had a brief romance with the dapper photographer Edgar Hanfstaengl. Sophie first met him three days after her engagement. While the bridegroom was away in Paris in July 1867 visiting the World Fair under the pseudonym of "Graf von Berg" (Count Mountain), Mistress bride was at home in Bavaria whispering sweet nothings to her "dear, most beloved friend", to whom she lamented in a letter: "Why did I come to know you just as I had chained myself to another?" The bonds were broken – and was it really her father who broke them? – In

König Ludwig II. von Bayern,
mit Allerhöchstdessen Braut,
Prinzessin Sophie, Herzogin in Bayern

Ein Grund für die Trennung könnte der Photograph Edgar Hanfstaengl gewesen sein, mit dem Sophie heimlich Liebesbriefe wechselte.

A cause of the break-up might have been the photographer Edgar Hanfstaengl, with whom Sophie secretly exchanged love letters.

Une raison de la séparation pourrait avoir été le photographe Edgar Hanfstaengl, avec lequel Sophie échangeait des lettres tendres en cachette.

Das Bild der 20-jährigen Braut, aufgenommen im Atelier Hanfstaengl.

A picture of the 20-year-old bride, taken in Hanfstaengl's photographic studio.

La photographie de la jeune fiancée, prise dans l'atelier Hanfstaengl.

Seite 41: Als Verlobte grüßen: König Ludwig II. von Bayern und Sophie, Herzogin in Bayern. Am 22. Januar 1867 wurde diese Verbindung geschlossen und acht Monate später wieder gelöst.

Page 41: Greetings from the engaged couple: King Ludwig II of Bavaria and Sophie Duchess of Bavaria. The bond was forged on 22 January 1867, but dissolved again eight months later.

Page 41 : Le roi Louis II de Bavière et Sophie, duchesse de Bavière: leurs fiançailles annoncées le 22 janvier 1867 furent rompues huit mois plus tard.

D'étranges fiançailles

Tout se passa de manière précipitée et certainement aussi irréfléchie. Ce jour de janvier 1867, le jeune roi, qui avait assisté à un bal, rentra à l'aube dans sa résidence, et au lieu de se coucher il se fit annoncer chez sa mère à six heures du matin pour la prier de demander pour lui au grand oncle Max, duc de Bavière, la main de sa fille Sophie. Une heure plus tard, les fiançailles étaient conclues et elles furent rendues publiques vers neuf heures du matin: le 22 janvier, Louis II roi de Bavière se fiança avec Sophie, duchesse de Bavière et sœur de l'impératrice d'Autriche Elisabeth. Les noces devaient être célébrées le 25 août, jour d'anniversaire du monarque. Une marche fut composée en l'honneur de la mariée, des médailles commémoratives furent gravées et un carrosse nuptial d'une valeur d'un million de florins fut commandé – mais le 25 août passa ainsi que d'autres dates fixées, et finalement le 7 octobre les fiançailles furent rompues à la demande du père de la fiancée.

Quelques jours avant les fiançailles, Sophie avait reçu une lettre du roi lui apprenant ce qu'elle savait déjà: « Le contenu principal de nos relations était toujours... le destin remarquable et émouvant de Richard Wagner. » Après la rupture, elle reçut une missive lui disant: « Chère Elsa! Ton père cruel nous arrache l'un à l'autre. Ton Henri pour l'éternité. » Peut-on rêver d'une telle union dans laquelle le fiancé choisit pour lui et sa future épouse les noms de personnages wagnériens?

La jeune duchesse n'aura pas trop souffert de la rupture, car au cours des fiançailles elle eut une brève liaison avec le fringant photographe Edgar Hanfstaengl rencontré pour la première fois trois jours après l'annonce des fiançailles. D'ailleurs pendant que le promis visitait l'exposition universelle de 1867 à Paris sous le pseudonyme de Graf von Berg, la promise folâtrait en Bavière avec son « cher et tendre ami » à qui elle se plaignit dans une lettre: « Pourquoi fallut-il que je te connaisse, maintenant que ma liberté est entravée? » Les chaînes furent rompues – est-ce vraiment le père qui le décida? – en novembre 1867, toutefois Louis écrit: « Dieu merci, l'épouvantable ne s'est pas accompli! (mon mariage aurait dû avoir lieu aujourd'hui). »

Im Sommer 1881 reiste König Ludwig mit dem von ihm verehrten Schauspieler Joseph Kainz in die Schweiz. Vor der Rückkehr nach Bayern ließ er sich zusammen mit seinem Gast in Luzern photographieren.

In the summer of 1881, King Ludwig travelled to Switzerland with Joseph Kainz, an actor he admired. Before returning to Bavaria, he had himself photographed together with his friend in Lucerne.

Au cours de l'été 1881, le roi fit un voyage en Suisse avec Joseph Kainz, un acteur qu'il vénérait. Il se fit photographier à Lucerne avec son invité avant de retourner en Bavière.

Kaiserin Elisabeth, gemalt von Franz Xaver Winterhalter, um 1865.

The Empress Elisabeth, painted by Franz Xaver Winterhalter, c. 1865.

L'impératrice Elisabeth, peinte par Franz Xaver Winterhalter, vers 1865.

Das Schloß Possenhofen am Starnberger See, Sommersitz der Familie von Herzog Max in Bayern.

Possenhofen Castle on Lake Starnberg, the Duke of Bavaria's family summer residence.

Le château de Possenhofen sur le lac de Starnberg, résidence d'été du duc Max, père d'Elisabeth.

Ludwig II. und seine Verlobte Herzogin Sophie auf dem Morgenritt, unvollendetes Gemälde von Franz Adam.

Ludwig II and his fiancée Duchess Sophie out on a morning ride, unfinished painting by Franz Adam.

Louis II et sa fiancée la duchesse Sophie pendant leur chevauchée matinale, toile inachevée de Franz Adam.

ich dich kennen lernen, nun da meine Freiheit in Fesseln geschlagen ist?" Die Fesseln wurden gelöst – und war es wirklich der Vater, der sie löste? –, im November 1867 aber schrieb Ludwig: „Gott sei gedankt, nicht ging das entsetzliche in Erfüllung! (mein Hochzeitstag sollte heute sein)."

Dem König, den Männer wohl ohnedies mehr interessierten als Frauen, blieb das Entsetzliche auch später erspart. Doch während die Trennung von Herzogin Sophie endgültig war, vertiefte sich in späteren Jahren die Verbindung des Bayernkönigs zu Sophies Schwester, der österreichischen Kaiserin Elisabeth. In ihr fand er eine verwandte Seele: Wie er seine Münchner Residenz, floh sie den Habsburger Hof in Wien, und was ihm Richard Wagners Musik, waren ihr die Verse von Heinrich Heine.

Einer ihrer gelegentlichen Treffpunkte war die im Starnberger See nahe von Sisis Elternschloß Possenhofen gelegene Roseninsel. Hier, wo er ein kleines Schlößchen besaß, fand König Ludwig im September 1885 ein Gedicht, das ihm die kaiserliche Cousine bei einem ihrer Besuche hinterlassen hatte:

Du Adler, dort hoch auf den Bergen,
Dir schickt die Möve der See
Einen Gruß von schäumenden Wogen
Hinauf zum ewigen Schnee...

Im Tode trafen sich die Schicksale der drei Wittelsbacher noch einmal – alle drei starben eines unnatürlichen Todes: Ludwig im Wasser (im Starnberger See), Sophie durch Feuer und Sisi durch Eisen (die Feile eines Attentäters). Eine Prophezeiung, so heißt es, habe diesen Tod durch die drei Elemente vorhergesagt.

November 1867 Ludwig wrote: "Thank God that the unthinkable came to nought! (today should have been my wedding day)."

Later, too, the king, who rather preferred men to women, remained spared of the unthinkable. Yet whereas the separation from Duchess Sophie was definitive, the Bavarian monarch's attachment in subsequent years to Sophie's sister, the Austrian Empress Elisabeth, developed and deepened. He found in her a kindred spirit – just as he had fled his seat in Munich, so did she the Habsburg court in Vienna, and what Richard Wagner's music was to him, so Heinrich Heine's verses were to her.

One occasional rendezvous was Rose Island in Lake Starnberg, near Sisi's parental castle of Possenhofen. Here, where King Ludwig himself had a small castle, he found in September 1885 a poem that his imperial cousin had left behind for him during one of her visits:

You eagle high up in the peaks
To you a seagull has tossed
A greeting from spumous breakers
Up to the permanent frost...

In death the fates of the three Wittelsbach scions once more became entwined – all three died unnatural deaths: Ludwig by water (in Lake Starnberg), Sophie by fire, and Sisi by steel (an assassin's file). The story goes that a prophecy foretold these deaths at the hand of the three elements.

Der Architekt Gottfried Semper sollte auf dem Isarhochufer in München eine neue Oper bauen.

The architect Gottfried Semper was to build a new opera house in Munich on the elevated bank of the River Isar.

L'architecte Gottfried Semper devait construire un nouvel opéra sur la rive haute de l'Isar à Munich.

In seinem Zürcher Exil bastelte Semper das Modell des zukünftigen Münchner Opernhauses. Im Juni 1867 stellte er es dem König vor, doch wurde dieser geniale Theaterbau nie verwirklicht.

In exile in Switzerland, Semper made a model of the future Munich opera house. In June 1867 it was shown to the king, but the inspired theatre building was never realized.

Exilé à Zurich, Semper dessina le modèle du futur opéra de Munich. Il le présenta au roi en juin 1867, mais ce bâtiment sensationnel ne fut jamais réalisé.

Louis II, qui du reste s'intéressait davantage aux hommes qu'aux femmes, put échapper sa vie durant au mariage exécré. Mais alors que la rupture avec la duchesse Sophie restait définitive, la relation du roi de Bavière avec la sœur de celle-ci, l'impératrice d'Autriche Elisabeth s'approfondit au cours des années qui suivirent. Il trouva en elle une âme sœur: tout comme il fuyait sa résidence de Munich, elle fuyait la cour des Habsbourg à Vienne, et les vers de Heine étaient pour elle ce que la musique de Wagner était pour lui.

Ils se rencontraient de temps en temps à l'Ile des Roses du lac de Starnberg, située près du château de Possenhofen appartenant aux parents de Sissi et où Louis II possédait un petit palais. C'est dans cet endroit qu'il trouva en septembre 1885 un poème que lui avait laissé sa cousine au cours d'une de ses visites:

> Toi l'aigle, haut sur la montagne,
> La mouette de la mer t'envoie
> Un salut de vagues écumantes
> Là-haut vers les neiges éternelles...

Les trois Wittelsbach connurent un destin tragique qui les réunit une fois encore – tous les trois périrent de mort violente: Louis par l'eau (dans le lac de Starnberg), Sophie par le feu et Sissi par le fer (le poignard d'un assassin). Une prophétie aurait annoncé cette mort par les trois éléments.

Ludwig II. als Postkartenmotiv: Der König in seinem Wintergarten.

Ludwig II as picture postcard motif – the king in his winter garden.

Louis II en motif de carte postale: le roi dans son jardin d'hiver.

Seite 50–51: Um 1880 malte Rudolf Wenig sein berühmtes Gemälde „Nächtliche Schlittenpartie Ludwigs II. von Neuschwanstein über den Schützensteig nach Linderhof".

Page 50–51: Around 1880 Rudolf Wenig painted his famous picture "Ludwig II's Nighttime Sleigh Ride from Neuschwanstein over the Schützensteig to Linderhof".

Page 50–51: Vers 1880, Rudolf Wenig peignit son célèbre tableau: « La randonnée nocturne en traîneau de Louis II, de Neuschwanstein à Linderhof, en passant par le Schützensteig ».

Für seinen Münchner Wintergarten hatte sich König Ludwig 1867 von dem Theatermaler Christian Jank als Hintergrundprospekte einen Mogulpalast und das Bergmassiv des Himalaja malen lassen. In dem etwa 70 m langen Raum mit seiner Glas-Eisenkonstruktion bildeten sie den Abschluß einer realistisch aufgebauten Seenlandschaft mit Palmen und einem Kahn.

Offensichtlich hat der wittelsbachische Regent an diesen exotischen Landschaften großen Gefallen gefunden, ließ er sie doch etliche Jahre später von Julius Lange in kleinerem Format für das Wohnzimmer seines Hauses auf dem Schachen kopieren.

In 1867 King Ludwig commissioned the theatre painter Christian Jank to paint a mogul palace and the Himalayan mountain massif as a backdrop for his Munich winter garden. The two subjects rounded off a realistically designed lakescape with palms and a boat in the roughly 70-metre-long (230 feet) room with its overarching steel and glass construction.

The Wittelsbach monarch evidently derived much pleasure from these exotic landscapes, for some years later he engaged Julius Lange to recreate them in a smaller format in the living quarters of his house on the Schachen mountain.

Pour son jardin d'hiver de Munich, Louis II avait fait peindre en arrière-plan un palais moghol et le massif de l'Himalaya par le décorateur de théâtre Christian Jank. Dans la salle longue de soixante-dix mètres avec sa construction de verre et d'acier, ils achevaient un paysage maritime réaliste agrémenté de palmiers et d'une barque.

Le souverain a manifestement éprouvé beaucoup de plaisir à contempler ces paysages exotiques, car il les fit copier des années plus tard en petit format par Julius Lange pour la salle de séjour de sa maison du Schachen.

Wäre er in seiner frühen Regierungszeit nicht daran gehindert worden, das Opernhaus auf dem rechten Isarufer zu bauen, hätte König Ludwig II. sich vielleicht häufiger in München aufgehalten. Nachdem sein Plan aber gescheitert war, ließ er sich auf dem Dach des nördlichen Residenzbaus einen Wintergarten errichten, richtete sich einige Wohnräume nach seinem Geschmack ein, lebte aber ansonsten die meiste Zeit des Jahres fernab seines Münchner Hofes, häufig auf Schloß Berg, doch auch in dem ihm aus Kindertagen vertrauten Hohenschwangau, in den drei großen Schlössern, die er sich in seinen zweiundzwanzig Regierungsjahren baute, oder auch auf einer der vielen Berghütten. Eines dieser ländlichen Häuser lag im Graswangtal, nahe dem Kloster Ettal.

Sein Vater hatte das kleine Bauernanwesen einst erworben und durch kleine Umbauten in ein Jagdhaus verwandeln lassen. Etwa ein Jahr nach dem verlorenen Krieg von 1866 und kurz vor seiner Entlobung ließ Ludwig II. in Erinnerung an einen Besuch in Versailles die Pläne für ein Schloß zeichnen, das dem Andenken Ludwig XIV. von Frankreich – und seinem Verständnis von Königtum – geweiht sein sollte.

Sie wurden immer wieder neu überarbeitet, und am Schluß sah der Bayernkönig wohl ein, daß sein Versailles in die gebirgige, rauhe Landschaft der Ammerberge nicht paßte. So gab er etwa zur Zeit des Deutsch-Französischen Krieges die Anweisung, die große Planung zurückzustellen und zunächst an das alte Haus, dem ehemaligen Linderhof, einige Räume anzubauen. Diesem ersten folgten noch etliche Anbauten, schließlich wurde das Jagdhaus abgerissen – an seiner Stelle ist schließlich ein Rokokoschloß im Stil der französischen Bourbonenkönige entstanden: das Schloß Linderhof.

Im Vestibül hat man zwar ein Reiterstandbild Ludwig XIV. aufgestellt, doch in den übrigen Räumen huldigte man vor allem Ludwig XV. und seinem Hofe: beispielsweise der königlichen Mätresse Dubarry, deren Porträt im „Rosa Kabinett" so angebracht wurde, daß der König bei seinem Diner im Speisezimmer zu ihr Blickkontakt hatte. Mit dieser Welt des 18. Jahrhunderts

Had King Ludwig II not been prevented early in his reign from building an opera house on the right bank of the Isar, he might have stayed in Munich more often. Instead he lived for most of the year in a variety of residences far from his Munich court. He stayed frequently at Berg Castle, sometimes at Hohenschwangau (which was familiar to him from his childhood days), occasionally at the three large castles that he built during his twenty-three years on the throne, and intermittently at one of his many mountain lodges. One of these rural retreats was in the Graswang valley, near the Ettal monastery.

His father had once acquired the little farmstead, converting it by degrees into a hunting lodge. About a year after the disastrous war of 1866, and shortly before his engagement, Ludwig II had plans drawn up – as a memento of a visit to Versailles – for a castle that was to be dedicated to the memory of France's Louis XIV and his idea of monarchy.

The plans were continually revised, and in the end the Bavarian king had to admit that his Versailles was not suited to the rugged landscape of the Ammerberg mountains. So at about the time of the Franco-Prussian war he gave instructions for the ambitious plan to be shelved and for some rooms to be temporarily added to the old house, the former Linderhof. This first extension was followed by many more until finally the hunting lodge was pulled down, to be replaced by a rococo castle in the style of the French Bourbon kings – the fairytale Linderhof Castle.

Although Ludwig installed an equestrian statue of Louis XIV in the vestibule, in the other rooms he paid homage above all to Louis XV and his court, for example to his royal mistress Dubarry, whose portrait was hung in the pink room in such a way that King Ludwig had eye contact with her when he had his evening meal in the dining room. He felt so closely associated with this 18th-century world that occasionally he had table places laid for the long-deceased members of the French court, making conversation during the meal with Queen Marie Antoinette, executed in 1793! As he did not want to

Der Spiegelsaal von Schloß Linderhof.

Linderhof Castle: the Hall of Mirrors.

La Galerie des Glaces du château de Linderhof.

Die vergoldete Floragruppe im Bassin vor der Hauptfassade von Linderhof.

The gilded Flora sculpture in the ornamental pool in front of Linderhof's main façade.

Le groupe de Flore doré dans le bassin situé devant la façade principale de Linderhof.

Seite 53: Inmitten der durch Carl von Effner geschaffenen Parkanlage: Schloß Linderhof.

Page 53: Linderhof Castle: in the middle of the grounds laid out by Carl von Effner.

Page 53: Le château de Linderhof se dresse au milieu d'un parc dessiné par Carl von Effner.

Auf dem reichverzierten, vergoldeten Deckel der königlichen Schreibmappe prangt das Monogramm Ludwigs II.

Ludwig II's monogram stands out on the richly decorated, gilded cover of the royal writing case.

Sur le couvercle doré, richement décoré du sous-main royal, le monogramme de Louis II.

Les maisons, les châteaux

Si on ne l'avait pas empêché de construire un opéra sur la rive droite de l'Isar au début de son règne, peut-être Louis II aurait-il séjourné plus souvent dans sa capitale. Il vivait en fait la plus grande partie de l'année loin de la Cour munichoise, souvent au château de Berg mais aussi à Hohenschwangau qu'il connaissait depuis son enfance, dans les trois grands palais qu'il fit édifier durant ses vingt-deux années de règne ou bien dans un de ses nombreux refuges de montagne. Un an après la défaite de 1866 et peu de temps avant la rupture de ses fiançailles, Louis II, se souvenant d'un séjour à Versailles, fit dessiner les plans d'un château dédié à la mémoire de Louis XIV.

Les plans furent remaniés de nombreuses fois, et finalement le roi de Bavière comprit que son Versailles n'était pas adapté au paysage montagneux et rude des Ammerberge. C'est ainsi qu'à l'époque de la guerre franco-allemande, il donna l'ordre d'ajourner les grands projets et d'abord d'agrandir la vieille ferme, l'ancien Linderhof. Finalement la vieille maison de chasse fut démolie – à sa place se dresse un château de contes de fées, le Linderhof, de style rococo d'inspiration française.

Si une statue équestre de Louis XIV se dresse dans le vestibule, c'est surtout à Louis XV et sa Cour que l'on rend hommage dans les autres pièces. Le roi, qui devait se dresser près d'une de ses maions transformée par son père en pavillon de chasse, dans la vallée du Graswang, près du monastère Ettal. Il se sentait si étroitement lié à cet univers XVIIIème, qu'il faisait même à l'occasion mettre le couvert pour des aristocrates depuis longtemps disparus.

La plus grande salle de ce château de taille plutôt modeste est la chambre à coucher. En effet, Sa Majesté (qui ne se levait jamais avant les premières heures de l'après-midi) était de l'avis qu'il s'agissait de la pièce la plus importante dans une résidence royale.

Comme le château, le parc de cinquante hectares fut créé en plusieurs étapes. Carl von Effner commença par tracer des jardins à la française de chaque côté de l'édifice. Plus tard il fit ériger sur une butte devant la

Deckengemälde im Spiegelsaal von Linderhof, das die Geburt der Venus zeigt. Das Inselschloß im Hintergrund verweist auf Herrenchiemsee.

Ceiling fresco in the Hall of Mirrors at Linderhof, which shows the Birth of Venus. The island castle in the background is a reference to Herrenchiemsee Castle.

Une Naissance de Vénus orne le plafond de la galerie des glaces de Linderhof. A l'arrière-plan, le château sur l'île renvoie au Herrenchiemsee.

Im Park von Schloß Linderhof liegt die Venusgrotte, eine künstliche Tropfsteinhöhle mit einem See, auf dem sich Ludwig herumrudern ließ. Je nach Laune des Königs konnte sie rot oder blau beleuchtet werden.

The Grotto of Venus, in the park surrounding Linderhof Castle, is an artificial dripstone cave with a lake inside. Ludwig used to row around this lake, which he could illuminate red or blue according to his mood.

La grotte de Vénus, dans le parc du château de Linderhof. Louis II se faisait promener en barque sur le lac de cette grotte artificielle qui pouvait être éclairée en bleu ou en rouge, au bon plaisir de Sa Majesté.

fühlte er sich so eng verbunden, daß er gelegentlich sogar für die längst verblichenen Mitglieder des französischen Hofes ein Gedeck auflegen ließ und mit der 1793 hingerichteten Königin Marie Antoinette während des Mahls Konversation machte. Weil er beim Essen aber seinen Bediensteten nicht begegnen wollte, ließ er sich ein Tischlein-deck-dich konstruieren, mit dem ihm diskret serviert wurde.

Der größte Raum in dem eher intimen Schloß ist das Schlafzimmer, das – obwohl bereits überproportional groß – zum Zeitpunkt von Ludwigs Tod gerade erweitert wurde. Denn, so meinte die Majestät (die immer erst am frühen Nachmittag aufzustehen pflegte), dies sei der wichtigste Raum in einer königlichen Residenz.

Die vielbesuchte, vielbewunderte Attraktion des großen Parks von Linderhof ist die von Carl von Effner abseits des Schlosses in eine künstlich geschaffene Höhle hineingebaute Venusgrotte. Auf Wunsch Ludwigs

encounter his servants while eating, he arranged for a magic table, a kind of "table séparée", to be constructed, at which he could be discreetly served. The largest room in this rather intimate castle is the bedchamber, which – although already enormous by any standards – was just being extended at the time of King Ludwig's death. The bedroom, so believed His Majesty (who was never in the habit of rising before the early afternoon), was the most important room in a royal residence.

The biggest attraction of Linderhof's extensive park, laid out by Carl von Effner, is the Venus Grotto. Here, at the request of Ludwig II, the grotto in the Hörsel mountain from the Tannhäuser myth was combined with the Blue Grotto of Capri. The cave with its dripstones and artificial lake was completed on 25 August 1877, the monarch's 32nd birthday. Everything connected with the Venus Grotto was lavishly constructed. Merely to work its illumination mechanism, one of

façade principale une rotonde avec une statue de Vénus, et plus loin aménager un petit bassin avec une fontaine de trente mètres de hauteur.

Effner agrémenta aussi d'un jeu d'eau la façade postérieure du château. Mais ce qui attire le plus les visiteurs dans le grand parc, c'est la grotte de Vénus, aménagée à l'écart dans une excavation artificielle et mélange de la grotte du Hörselberg originaire du mythe de Tannhäuser et de la Grotte bleue de Capri, ainsi que le voulut Louis II. Le 25 août 1877, trente-deuxième anniversaire du monarque, vit l'achèvement de cette grotte à stalactites et stalagmites et lac artificiel, dont l'éclairage nécessita l'installation d'une des premières centrales électriques bavaroises. Cet univers de rêve coûta à lui seul un million deux cent mille marks.

L'aménagement du parc n'en était pas pour autant terminé. En hommage à l'opéra wagnérien, sous le som-

Seite 58: Bei seinem Besuch auf der Pariser Weltausstellung 1867 bestaunte König Ludwig den Maurischen Kiosk. Neun Jahre später kaufte er ihn für die Parkanlage in Linderhof.

Page 58: Visiting the Paris World Fair in 1867, King Ludwig was much taken by the Moorish pavilion. Nine years later he bought the kiosk for the grounds of Linderhof.

Page 58 : Lors de sa visite à l'exposition universelle de Paris en 1867, Louis II admira le kiosque maure. Neuf ans plus tard, il l'achetait pour le parc de Linderhof.

Mittelpunkt und größte Attraktion des Maurischen Kiosks ist der in Paris angefertigte Pfauenthron.

Centrepiece and greatest attraction of the Moorish kiosk is the peacock throne, produced in Paris.

Le Trône aux paons, réalisé à Paris, est l'objet le plus captivant et le plus admiré du kiosque maure.

wurde dabei die aus der Tannhäuser-Sage stammende Grotte im Hörselberg mit der Blauen Grotte von Capri kombiniert. Am 32. Geburtstag des Monarchen, am 25. August 1877, war diese Höhle mit den Tropfsteinen und dem künstlichen See vollendet.

Weil aber alles sehr aufwendig gebaut und für den Betrieb der Beleuchtungsmechanik auch noch eines der ersten Elektrizitätswerke Bayerns (eine allerdings sehr kleine Anlage) installiert wurde, kostete allein diese unterirdische Traum- und Kulissenwelt in den wechselnden Farben Rot und Blau 1,2 Millionen Mark. Der Ausbau der Parkwelt war damit aber noch nicht abgeschlossen. Im Andenken an die wagnersche Opernwelt war unter der Kreuzspitze, und damit in einigem Abstand zum Schloß, die Einsiedelei des Gurnemanz („Parzifal") und in der Nachbarschaft dazu die Hundinghütte („Walküre") errichtet worden. In dieser Abgeschiedenheit stand noch – als Kontrastprogramm zur Alpenwelt – ein Marokkanisches Haus, zu dem das in der Nähe der Venusgrotte gelegene Maurische Haus paßte.

Zu Beginn des Jahres 1869 hatte Ludwig seiner ehemaligen Erzieherin, der Baronin Leonrod, geschrieben: „Oh, es ist notwendig, sich solche Paradiese zu schaffen, solche poetischen Zufluchtsorte, wo man auf einige Zeit die schaudershafte Zeit, in der wir leben, vergessen kann" – und viele Jahre lang war er von da an damit beschäftigt, in der unwirtlichen Gegend des Ammergebirges der Natur eines dieser Paradiese abzutrotzen. Linderhof war zuletzt das einzige der drei Ludwig-Schlösser, das fertiggestellt wurde und in dem der Märchenkönig sich häufig aufhielt. Und von hier aus unternahm er in seinem vergoldeten Schlitten jene nächtlichen Fahrten, die in der Phantasie der Menschen weiterleben.

Der Preis, den er für seine Paradiese zahlen mußte, war reichlich hoch und wurde zuletzt auch als einer der Gründe für seine Entmündigung angegeben. Zwar wies die Zivilliste dem König ein Jahreseinkommen von 4,2 Millionen Mark zu, doch über einen großen Teil des Geldes konnte er nicht frei verfügen; es mußte für die Hofhaltung, die Hofbediensteten und andere feste Posten ausgegeben werden. Die Ausgaben überstiegen die Einnahmen schließlich in solchem Maße, daß auch die Zuschüsse aus Vermögensreserven und aus Bismarcks Welfenfonds nicht ausreichten, den königlichen Privatetat auszugleichen. Bereits in den frühen 8oer Jahren waren die Schulden auf 8,25 Mill. Mark angewachsen.

Bavaria's first power stations (albeit only a very small one) had to be built. The upshot was that this subterranean theatrical dreamworld alone, with its alternating red and blue colours, cost a cool 1.2 million marks.

However, this was not the end of the development of Ludwig's Linderhof "theme park". As a memento of the Wagnerian opera world, he erected Gurnemanz's ("Parsifal's") hermitage and near it the Hunding hut ("Valkyrie") below the Kreuzspitze and hence some distance away from the castle. Two other buildings stood in this secluded spot, forming quite a contrast to the Bavarian Alpine surroundings – a Moroccan house and, in the same idiom, a Moorish pavilion near the Venus Grotto. In early 1869 King Ludwig had written to his former governess, Baroness Leonrod: "Oh, it is necessary to create such paradises, such poetic refuges, where for a moment one can forget the dreadful times in which we live" – and from that time on he was preoccupied with wringing from nature one of these paradises on the rugged, inhospitable slopes of the Ammer mountains. In the end Linderhof was the only one of the three King Ludwig castles that was ever finished and where the Bavarian fairytale king stayed regularly. And it was from here, in his golden sleigh, that he took those night-time rides which live on in people's imaginations.

The price that Ludwig had to pay for his castle paradises was, of course, very high and in the end was cited as one of the arguments for his being certified as incapable of managing his own affairs. Although the civil list allocated to the king an annual income of 4.2 million marks, he was not free to spend a large part of this because he had to pay for upkeep of the court, court servants and other fixed costs. In the end his expenses exceeded his income to such an extent that even subsidies from capital reserves and from Bismarck's Guelphic Fund were not enough to balance the royal private budget. By the early 1880s, Ludwig's debts had grown to 8.25 million marks.

The plans for the royal Bavarian Versailles in the Ammer valley behind Ettal were still being busily drawn up when Ludwig II conceived the idea of returning to places familiar to him from his childhood. On a mountain top near Hohenschwangau Castle he wanted to pay homage to the Middle Ages. In May 1868 he wrote to his soul mate Richard Wagner: "I intend to have the old Hohenschwangau castle ruin near the Pöllat ravine

met du Kreuzspitze, on avait construit l'ermitage du Gournemans (« Parsifal ») et dans son voisinage la hutte de Hunding (« Walkyrie »). Dans cet endroit isolé se dressait aussi une maison marocaine, pendant de la maison maure qui se trouvait près de la grotte de Vénus.

Linderhof fut le seul des trois châteaux du roi Louis à être achevé.

Assurément, le prix qu'il dut payer pour ses paradis fut très élevé, d'ailleurs les sommes dépensées furent l'une des raisons de sa mise en tutelle. Quand on tira le trait final en 1886 (entre-temps le roi était mort et le mark avait remplacé le florin), si plus de trois millions et demi étaient prévus au total, on avait dépensé en réalité huit millions quatre cent mille marks. L'écart était encore plus flagrant en ce qui concerne le château de Herrenchiemsee, pour lequel au cours des années 1873 à 1886 on avait évalué les frais à un peu plus de cinq millions six cent quarante mille marks, mais dépensé seize millions cinq cent soixante-dix mille marks.

La liste civile du roi prévoyait un revenu annuel de quatre millions deux cent mille marks, mais il ne pouvait disposer librement d'une grande partie de cette somme qui servait à couvrir l'entretien de la Cour, les salaires des serviteurs et autres frais fixes. Les dépenses finirent par dépasser les recettes, de telle sorte que même les sommes allouées par les réserves du patrimoine et le fonds des Guelfes de Bismarck ne suffisaient plus à équilibrer le budget privé du roi.

Celui-ci ne commit pas seulement l'erreur d'être par trop dispendieux (il s'agissait d'ailleurs de son argent et non de celui de la caisse publique), il était également peu commode sur le plan politique. Il finit donc par se trouver des hommes pour vouloir le remplacer par son oncle, le prince Léopold.

Les plans du Versailles bavarois dans la vallée de la Ammer derrière Ettal faisaient encore l'objet d'études serrées, quand Louis II projeta de retourner à l'endroit qui lui était familier depuis son enfance. En mai 1868, il écrit à son alter ego Richard Wagner : « J'ai l'intention de faire reconstruire le vieux château fort en ruines de Hohenschwangau près de la gorge de Pöllat dans le style des anciens châteaux des chevaliers allemands ». Mais ce nouvel édifice, qui ne reçut le nom de Neuschwanstein qu'après la mort du souverain, ne fut jamais achevé.

Il fut cependant ouvert aux visiteurs dès le 1er août 1886, pour que le peuple voie de ses yeux le degré de

Seite 60 : Auf einem schmalen Höhenrücken nahe dem Schloß Hohenschwangau baute Ludwig Neuschwanstein als eine Burg „im echten Styl der alten deutschen Ritterburgen".

Page 60 : King Ludwig built Neuschwanstein Castle on a narrow mountain ridge as a real castle "in the authentic style of the strongholds of the German knights of old".

Page 60 : Sur un étroit sommet montagneux, à proximité du château de Hohenschwangau, Louis II fit construire Neuschwanstein, qui reprend le style « des anciens châteaux forts des chevaliers allemands ».

Der im byzantinischen Stil gestaltete Thronsaal
von Neuschwanstein.

Neuschwanstein's throne room created in the
Byzantine style.

La salle du trône de Neuschwanstein, agencée
dans le style byzantin.

Im vierten Obergeschoß, über den Wohnräumen der Majestät, entstand in Erinnerung an den Besuch auf der Wartburg und in Anlehnung an das Bühnenbild einer Münchner Tannhäuser-Inszenierung als geheimer Mittelpunkt des ganzen Schloßprojektes der Sängersaal.

King Ludwig built the minstrels' hall on the fourth floor, above his personal living quarters. Considered the secret centrepiece of the whole castle project, it recalled his visit to Wartburg Castle and was based on the stage set of a Munich production of "Tannhäuser".

Au quatrième étage, au-dessus des appartements du roi, le cœur secret du château, la Salle des chanteurs, réminiscence d'une visite à la Wartburg avec des influences des décors du Tannhäuser munichois.

Im Schwan, der in Hohenschwangau wie in Neuschwanstein so vielfach dargestellt ist – wie zum Beispiel in dieser Majolika-Blumenvase – huldigte Ludwig dem einst hier ansässigen Rittergeschlecht der Schwangauer und Wagners Lohengrin.

At Hohenschwangau and Neuschwanstein there are numerous swan representations, such as here in this majolica flower vase. With the swan figure, Ludwig paid homage to the lineage of Schwangau knights, who once resided in the locality, as well as to Wagner's Lohengrin.

Avec le cygne, que l'on retrouve si souvent représenté à Hohenschwangau comme à Neuschwanstein – par exemple sur ce vase en majolique – Louis II rend hommage à l'ancienne famille des chevaliers de Schwangau qui résidait ici et au Lohengrin de Wagner.

Es wurde noch eifrig an den Plänen für das königlich-bayerische Versailles im Ammertal hinter Ettal gezeichnet, als Ludwig II. den Plan faßte, an die Stätte zurückzukehren, die ihm aus seinen Kindertagen vertraut war: Auf einer Bergkuppe nahe von Schloß Hohenschwangau wollte er dem Mittelalter huldigen. Im Mai 1868 schrieb er an seinen Seelenfreund Richard Wagner: „Ich habe die Absicht, die alte Burgruine Hohenschwangau bei der Pöllatschlucht neu aufbauen zu lassen im echten Styl der alten deutschen Ritterburgen". In drei Jahren, so hoffte er, würde der Bau, dieser „würdige Tempel für den göttlichen Freund", vollendet sein.

Doch diese „Neue Burg Hohenschwangau", die erst nach dem Tod des Königs den Namen „Neuschwanstein" erhielt, wurde nie zu Ende gebaut. In den Rechnungsbüchern der Kabinettskasse aber war nachzulesen, daß dennoch Ausgaben in Höhe von 6,18 Millionen Mark angefallen waren.

Um dem Volke den Grad geistiger Verwirrung, den der König angeblich erreicht habe, deutlich vor Augen zu führen – und so gleichsam die Entmündigung zu rechtfertigen –, wurde bereits am 1. August 1886 das Schloß Neuschwanstein zur Besichtigung freigegeben. Die beabsichtigte Wirkung ist nicht eingetreten. Im Gegenteil. Die über einer alten Ruine errichtete Burg Neuschwanstein wurde zur berühmtesten Touristenattraktion des Landes, und im April 1998 wurde in ihr der 40 millionste Besucher gezählt.

Dabei hatte Ludwig II. zunächst wohl nichts anderes gewünscht als eine freie Nachbildung der Wartburg bei Eisenach, die er im Juni 1868 zusammen mit seinem (wenige Jahre später geisteskrank gewordenen) Bruder Otto besucht hatte. Doch wie bei allen Bauprojekten des Königs wurden die Pläne immer wieder neu gezeichnet. Schließlich entstand eine Huldigung an den Sänger Tannhäuser und an Richard Wagner sowie eine Demonstration seines Verständnisses von königlicher Würde. So wurden der Sänger- und der im Stile eines byzantinischen Kirchenraumes gestaltete Thronsaal zum Mittelpunkt dieser gotischen Burg aus dem späten 19. Jahrhundert.

Dem König und seinen Architekten mag es manchmal schwer gefallen sein, bei den vielen parallellaufenden Projekten den Überblick nicht zu verlieren. So wurde am späteren Schloß Linderhof bereits gebaut, als in der Münchner Residenz die Königswohnung neu ein-

rebuilt in the authentic style of the old German knights' castles." The building, this "dignified temple for a divine friend", would, he hoped, be finished in three years. But the "New Hohenschwangau Castle", which became known as "Neuschwanstein" only after the king's death, was never completed. Despite this, the cabinet treasury account books showed that expenses were incurred to the tune of 6.18 million marks.

In order to bring home to the people just how demented the king had become – and at the same time justify his certification – the opening of Neuschwanstein Castle to visitors was brought forward to 1 August 1886. But the ploy backfired. Neuschwanstein Castle, built on top of an old ruin, became the most famous tourist attraction in the country – by April 1998 it had notched up its 40 millionth visitor. Initially, Ludwig II had wanted nothing more than to roughly recreate Wartburg Castle near Eisenach, which he had visited in June 1868 with his brother Otto (soon to become mentally ill). But, as with all the king's architectural projects, the plans were continually recast. In the end it turned into a homage to the singer Tannhäuser – and to Richard Wagner – and into a demonstration of his understanding of regal grandeur. Thus the minstrels' hall and the throne room, built in the style of a Byzantine church room, became the focal point of this late 19th-century Gothic castle.

Sometimes it must have been difficult for the king and his architects to keep track of the many projects running side by side. Work was already in progress at what was to become Linderhof Castle at the same time that the king's quarters were being refurbished in his Munich residence and the foundation stone was being laid on the 1866-metre-high (6122 feet) Schachen peak in the Wetterstein mountains for a king's house in the Swiss style (with partly oriental interior decoration). Then, on 5 September 1869, five weeks after work started on the Schachen, the foundation stone was also laid for Neuschwanstein Castle. On top of all this, in 1873 the king acquired – mainly for ecological reasons – the monastery island of Herrenchiemsee, and since 1878 work had been continuing there on the Wittelsbach Versailles that in the 1860s had first been planned as "Meicost Ettal".

Herrenchiemsee Castle was still far from finished when work was suspended, the already completed structure of one wing was torn down, and the foundations of

Die hohen Schulden und schließlich der Tod des Königs haben die Fertigstellung von Schloß und Parkanlagen verhindert. Noch wenige Jahre vor dem Ende der Bauarbeiten war aber vor der Westseite von Herrenchiemsee der Latonabrunnen mit seinen wasserspeienden Fröschen eingeweiht worden.

The king's huge debts and finally his death put paid to any hope of the castle and its grounds being completed. However, a few years before work was halted, the Latona fountain with its water-spouting frogs was inaugurated on the west side of Herrenchiemsee.

Le château et les jardins n'ont pu être achevés à cause des dettes élevées et, finalement, la mort du souverain. Mais juste quelques années avant la fin des travaux, on avait inauguré devant la façade occidentale de Herrenchiemsee la fontaine de Latone et ses grenouilles d'où jaillit l'eau.

Seite 66–67: Auf einer ursprünglich von Mönchen bewohnten Insel mitten im Chiemsee wollte König Ludwig II. mit einer freien Nachbildung des Schlosses von Versailles König Ludwig XIV. von Frankreich huldigen.

Page 66–67: On an island, originally inhabited by monks, in the middle of Lake Chiem, Ludwig II wanted to pay homage to France's King Louis XIV with a free recreation of the Palace of Versailles.

Pages 66–67 : En construisant une imitation libre de Versailles sur une île du lac de Chiem, occupée à l'origine par des moines, Louis II voulait rendre hommage au Roi-Soleil.

Nach dem Latonabrunnen ließ der König zwei Jahre vor seinem Tod in den näher beim Schloß gelegenen beiden Wasserbecken zwei hochaufragende Felstürme mit einer Fortuna- und einer Famagruppe errichten. Die beiden Brunnen – unser Bild zeigt den Fortunabrunnen – wurden bald nach dem Tod Ludwigs II. zerstört und sind erst jüngst, nach einhundert Jahren, wieder restauriert worden.

After the Latona fountain, and two years before his death, the king commissioned for the two pools situated closer to the castle two soaring rock towers with Fortuna and Fama statues. These two fountains – the illustration shows the Fortuna fountain – were destroyed soon after Ludwig's death and have only recently, a century later, been restored.

Deux ans avant sa mort, après la fontaine de Latone, Louis II fit édifier dans les deux bassins situés près du château deux hautes tours de pierre, avec des statues de la Fortune et de la Renommée. Les deux fontaines – l'illustration montre la fontaine de la Fortune – furent détruites peu de temps après la disparition du souverain, elles viennent d'être restaurées, un siècle plus tard.

folie atteint par le roi – qui justifiait la mise en tutelle. Or c'est devenu depuis le site le plus célèbre du pays, il a fêté son quarante millionième visiteur en avril 1998.

Pourtant, Louis II ne souhaitait au départ rien d'autre qu'une imitation libre de la Wartburg près d'Eisenach. Mais comme tous les autres projets architecturaux du roi, les plans furent sans cesse remaniés. Le résultat final est un hommage au chanteur Tannhäuser – et à Richard Wagner – ainsi qu'une démonstration de sa conception de la dignité royale.

Le roi et ses architectes ont peut-être parfois eu du mal à garder une vue d'ensemble de tous les projets entrepris parallèlement. Ainsi, cinq semaines après la pose de la première pierre sur le mont Schachen de la maison suisse, le château de Neuschwanstein était mis en chantier (le 5 sept. 1869), et après qu'en 1873 le roi eut acquis – l'île-monastère de Herrenchiemsee, la construction du Versailles wittelsbachien commença en 1878.

L'édifice devait « fêter la mémoire du roi Louis XIV ». Au centre des préoccupations, la chambre à coucher du Roi-Soleil. Si Louis le Deuxième, roi de Bavière, avait prévu quatre-vingt-dix mètres carrés pour sa chambre blanche, bleu et or, celle de sa Majesté Louis le Quatorzième, qui en avait fait « le sanctuaire de la royauté » – l'étiquette y réglant les cérémonies du Lever et du Coucher – comptait cent soixante huit mètres carrés. Devant cette pièce, sur le côté ouest du château de Herrenchiemsee tourné vers le parc, Louis II fit reproduire la Galerie des Glaces du château de Versailles, mais ici c'est la copie, longue de quatre-vingt-dix-huit mètres, qui est plus vaste que l'original. Cette salle d'apparat est éclairée par dix-huit cents bougies sur des torchères, et des portes de verre laissent passer la lumière; dans sa chambre, le roi souhaitait, en plus des nombreuses bougies, un éclairage supplémentaire sous la forme d'une boule de verre bleue illuminée par la flamme d'une bougie. Sa Majesté prêtant une attention pointilleuse à chaque détail de l'aménagement intérieur, il fallut au peintre de décors de théâtre Otto Stöger un an et demi de travail pour trouver le bleu correspondant aux désirs du commanditaire.

Le château de Herrenchiemsee était loin d'être terminé quand les travaux furent interrompus, une aile latérale dont la maçonnerie était terminée, abattue, et une seconde aile latérale maçonnée dans les fondations, nivelée. Le Versailles bavarois avait déjà englouti plus de

In Lebensgröße hat Elisabeth Ney den König in Gips modelliert. Das vom Bildhauer Friedrich Ochs in Marmor umgesetzte Standbild, das für das von Ludwig II. erbaute Polytechnikum (heute Technische Universität) bestimmt war, kam in das nur im Rohbau fertiggestellte nördliche Treppenhaus von Herrenchiemsee.

Elisabeth Ney's lifesize model of the king was done in plaster of Paris. The sculptor Friedrich Ochs then reworked the statue in marble. Originally intended for the polytechnic (today a technical university) established by Ludwig II, the piece came by a circuitous route to stand on Herrenchiemsee's unfinished northern staircase.

Elisabeth Ney a modelé le roi en plâtre grandeur nature. La statue en pied que le sculpteur Friedrich Ochs réalisa en marbre d'après ce modèle était destinée à l'Ecole Polytechnique construite par Louis II (aujourd'hui Université Technique) ; elle parvint dans l'escalier nord, seulement maçonné, du château de Herrenchiemsee.

Das mit farbigem Marmor verkleidete südliche Treppenhaus ist der „Escalier des Ambassadeurs" nachempfunden, deren Versailler Vorbild bereits im 18. Jahrhundert abgerissen wurde und König Ludwig II. nur aus Stichen bekannt war.

The southern staircase, faced with coloured marble, recreates the "Escalier des Ambassadeurs". The original model in Versailles had already been demolished in the 18th century, and King Ludwig II knew it only from engravings.

L'escalier sud revêtu de marbre coloré est une imitation de l'Escalier des Ambassadeurs du château de Versailles, démoli au 18e siècle, et dont Louis II ne connaissait que des gravures.

gerichtet und auf dem 1866 Meter hohen Schachen im Wettersteingebirge der Grundstein für das Königshaus im Schweizer Stil (mit zum Teil orientalischer Inneneinrichtung) gelegt wurde.

Fünf Wochen nach dem Baubeginn auf dem Schachen wurde am 5. 9. 1869 auch der Grundstein für Neuschwanstein gelegt, und nachdem der König 1873 vornehmlich aus ökologischen Gründen die Klosterinsel Herrenchiemsee erworben hatte, wurde dort seit 1878 an jenem wittelsbachischen Versailles gebaut, das in den 6oer Jahren als „Meicost Ettal" erstmals geplant worden war.

Das Schloß Herrenchiemsee war noch weit von seiner Fertigstellung entfernt, als die Bauarbeiten eingestellt, ein im Rohbau bereits errichteter Seitentrakt abgerissen und ein anderer in den Grundfesten gemauerter zweiter Seitentrakt eingeebnet wurde. Mehr als sechs Millionen Mark waren für das bayerische Versailles bezahlt, als König Ludwig Thron und Macht verlor.

Die Minister in München hatten geglaubt, die drei Schlösser würden das Volk der Bayern davon überzeugen, daß der König geisteskrank gewesen und Bayern nur durch dessen Absetzung vor dem finanziellen Ruin zu bewahren gewesen sei (obwohl die Baukosten den Staatshaushalt gar nicht belastet hatten).

Die Besucher der Königsschlösser sahen und sehen dies freilich anders. Im übrigen entsprang das Bauprogramm zwar einer königlichen Laune, es war aber auch ein großes Arbeitsbeschaffungsprogramm, das Geld in

An die Decke seines Ankleidezimmers in Herrenchiemsee ließ sich Ludwig – der seeumflossenen Lage des Schlosses angemessen – den Meergott Poseidon malen. Er selbst hat das Meer nie gesehen.

At Herrenchiemsee Ludwig had the sea-god Poseidon painted on the ceiling of his dressing room, an idea in keeping with the castle's setting in the middle of a lake. He himself never saw the sea.

Sur le plafond de son cabinet d'habillage du château de Herrenchiemsee, situé au milieu d'un lac, le roi de Bavière a fait peindre le dieu marin Poséidon. Lui-même ne vit jamais la mer.

another wing were levelled. By the time that King Ludwig lost his throne and power, more than six million marks had been spent on the Bavarian Versailles. Ludwig's ministers in Munich had thought that the three castles would convince the Bavarian populace that the king was mentally unbalanced and that Bavaria was only to be saved from financial ruin by deposing him (although the construction costs had not burdened the state coffers at all). Visitors to the royal castles saw and have continued to see the matter differently. The architectural programme may have been the result of a kingly whim, but it was also a major job-creation scheme that channelled money to poor and remote regions, which was another reason why the people loved their king.

Scarcely less important was the fact that all the commissions going to wood carvers, gilders, painters and gold embroiderers brought about a great resurgence

six millions de marks quand le roi perdit son trône et son autorité.

Les ministres de Munich avaient cru que les trois châteaux convaincraient la population de la folie du roi, et qu'elle comprendrait que seule son abdication pouvait sauver la Bavière de la ruine. Mais les visiteurs voyaient à vrai dire les choses d'un autre œil, et la popularité de Louis II était grande. Tout né qu'il fut d'un caprice royal, le programme de construction apportait pas moins du travail à beaucoup de gens dans des régions isolées et pauvres. Louis II avait manifesté un jour le désir que l'on fasse sauter ses châteaux après sa mort. Il ne fallait pas que ses créations lui survivent, que ses rêves architecturaux soient profanés. Personne n'a songé à détruire Linderhof, Neuschwanstein ou Herrenchiemsee, et ainsi vit en eux le souvenir d'un des plus fascinants souverains de la Bavière, le dernier prince romantique.

Die Majestät wartet in Schloß Linderhof, daß das Tischlein-deck-dich mit Speisen gefüllt vor ihm erscheine...

In Linderhof Castle, His Majesty waits for his "magic table" to appear before him laden with food...

Dans sa salle à manger du château de Linderhof, Sa Majesté attend que sa petite table apparaisse, recouverte de mets comme par enchantement...

... und dieser Mechanismus transportierte den Tisch.

... and this mechanism transported the table to him.

... c'est ce mécanisme qui transportait la table.

Seite 74: Georg Schachinger hat dieses repräsentative Bild Ludwigs II. im Ornat des Georgiritterordens erst 1887, ein Jahr nach dem Tod des Königs, vollendet.

Page 74: Georg Schachinger only finished this imposing picture of Ludwig II in the regalia of the Order of the Knights of St George in 1887, a year after the king's death.

Page 74 : Georg Schachinger n'a terminé ce tableau d'apparat représentant Louis II en tenue de Grand Maître de l'ordre des Chevaliers de Saint-Georges qu'en 1887, un an après la mort du roi.

Seite 75: Der festlichste Raum von Herrenchiemsee ist der dem Versailler Vorbild nachgebildete Spiegelsaal mit seinen 1800 Kerzen und einer Länge von beinahe 100 Metern.

Page 75: Almost 100 metres (330 feet) long, and lit by 1800 candles, the most magnificent room in Herrenchiemsee is the Hall of Mirrors, modelled on the one in Versailles.

Page 75 : Cette imitation de la Galerie des Glaces de Versailles, longue de près de cent mètres et éclairée de mille huit cents bougies est la salle la plus solennelle, la plus impressionnante de Herrenchiemsee.

Das Speisezimmer in Schloß Herrenchiemsee.

The dining room in Herrenchiemsee.

La salle à manger à Herrenchiemsee.

abgelegene, arme Regionen brachte. Auch deswegen liebten die Menschen ihren König. Kaum weniger wichtig war, daß die Aufträge an Schnitzer, Vergolder, Maler oder Goldstickerinnen dem Münchner Kunsthandwerk einen großen Aufschwung brachten, der weit in die Prinzregentenzeit hineinreichte und im Münchner Jugendstil einen weiteren Höhepunkt erreichte.

Einst hatte Ludwig II. den Wunsch ausgesprochen, man sollte die Schlösser nach seinem Tode sprengen. Seine Schöpfungen sollten ihn nicht überleben, seine architektonischen Träume sollten nicht profaniert werden. Niemand hat daran gedacht, Linderhof, Neuschwanstein oder Herrenchiemsee zu zerstören, und so lebt in ihnen die Erinnerung an einen der faszinierendsten Herrscher Bayerns, an einen Märchenkönig weiter.

in Munich craftsmanship that lasted well into the prince regency and reached a further highpoint in the "Jugendstil" movement in the Bavarian capital. Ludwig II had once expressed a desire that the castles should be blown up after his death. His creations were not to outlive him, his architectural dreams should not be profaned. But no one has ever contemplated destroying Linderhof, Neuschwanstein or Herrenchiemsee, and so the memory of one of Bavaria's most fascinating rulers, of a fairytale king, lives on in them.

Seite 78: „Cosa rara", ein Lieblingspferd Ludwigs, 1872 vor dem Königshäuschen, an dessen Stelle das Schloß Linderhof steht.

Page 78: "Cosa Rara", one of Ludwig's favourite horses in 1872 in front of the king's hunting lodge, where Linderhof Castle now stands.

Page 78 : « Cosa rara », le cheval favori de Louis II, en 1872 devant la maisonnette qui a cédé la place au château de Linderhof.

Auf dem 1866 m hohen Schachen wurde ab 1869 das Königshaus errichtet.

The building of this royal mountain lodge on the 1866-metre-high (6122 feet) Schachen peak, began in 1869.

En 1869, la maison royale fut mise en chantier sur le Schachen haut de 1866 m.

Der Theatermaler Christian Jank lieferte diesen Entwurf für eine Burg auf dem Falkenstein. Es war der letzte Bau, den der König in Auftrag gab, der aber nie ausgeführt wurde.

The theatre painter Christian Jank produced this sketch for a castle on the Falkenstein. It was the last architectural commission the king was to give, which was, however, never carried out.

Le peintre de décors de théâtre Christian Jank livra le projet d'un château fort sur le Falkenstein. Ce fut le dernier édifice commandité par Louis II, et qui ne fut jamais mis en œuvre.

Neben mehreren schlicht eingerichteten Zimmern gibt es im ersten Stock des Schachenhauses einen türkischen Raum mit einem Springbrunnen.

Besides several simply furnished rooms, the Schachen house has a Turkish room with a fountain on the first floor.

A côté de quelques pièces sobrement meublées, le premier étage de la maison de Schachen abrite un bain turc agrémenté d'une fontaine.

Ein rätselhafter Tod

Am 8. Juni 1886 legten vier angesehene Nervenärzte ein in großer Eile angefertigtes Gutachten vor, und obwohl sie den königlichen Patienten gar nicht untersucht hatten, fällten sie ihr Urteil: „Wir erklären einstimmig: Se. Majestät sind in sehr weit fortgeschrittenem Stadium seelengestört, und zwar leiden Allerhöchstdieselben an jener Form von Geisteskrankheit, die den Irrenärzten aus Erfahrung wohl bekannt, mit dem Namen Paranoia (Verrücktheit) bezeichnet wird…"

Der Vorsitzende des Ministerrates, Freiherr von Lutz hörte dies gern, denn nun konnte er, dem eine Entlassung durch König Ludwig II. drohte, Prinz Luitpold die Entmündigung des Königs vorschlagen – und gleichzeitig sein Verbleiben im Amt sichern.

Einen ersten Versuch, die Majestät in Schloß Neuschwanstein gefangenzunehmen, hatten in der Nacht vom 9. zum 10. Juni die aus der Umgebung herbeigerufenen Gendarme und Feuerwehrmänner verhin-

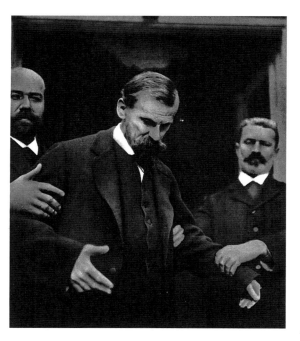

An enigmatic death

On 8 June 1886, four respected neurologists produced a hastily prepared report, and although they had at no point examined the royal patient, pronounced their judgement: "We unanimously declare His Majesty to be in an advanced state of mental instability and to be suffering from that form of mental illness which the psychiatrists from long experience call by the name of paranoia (madness)…" This was music to the ears of Baron von Lutz, who presided over Ludwig's council of ministers, because now, threatened as he was with dismissal by the king, he could suggest to Prince Luitpold certifying the monarch, at the same time ensuring that he himself would remain in office.

A first attempt to take His Majesty captive in Neuschwanstein Castle had been thwarted on the night of 9/10 June by gendarmes and firemen called in from the surrounding area. At a second attempt the so-called "custody commission" from Munich was more successful. Offering no resistance, the king allowed himself to be arrested and conducted to a waiting carriage. He asked the person medically overseeing the operation, the highly respected Dr Gudden (and many Bavarians later wondered whether a person allegedly as deranged as the king would be capable of so speaking): "How can you declare me insane? After all, you have never seen or examined me before."

At midday 12 June the king arrived at Berg Castle on Lake Starnberg with his doctors and guards, but by the evening of the following day, Whit Sunday, he was dead. Around 6.30 or 6.45 p.m. he had left his royal castle, which had been converted into a lunatic asylum, in order to take a walk in the company of Dr Gudden, and about 10.30 p.m. the bodies of the two men were found drifting in the lake twenty to twenty-five metres from the shore.

The circumstances of these deaths remain a great mystery, endlessly debated yet still unsolved to the present day. Had the king intended to flee, only to be prevented by Dr Gudden? Cousin Sisi, it is said, had made preparations to abduct Ludwig to Tyrol, leaving carriages at intervals outside the castle grounds ready to

Une mort mystérieuse

Le 8 juin 1886, huit neurologues réputés présentèrent une expertise rédigée à la hâte, et bien qu'ils n'aient pas examiné le patient royal, ils jugèrent à l'unanimité que Sa Majesté souffrait d'une maladie psychique à un stade très avancé, notamment une forme de maladie mentale bien connue des médecins des fous, celle qui porte le nom de paranoïa....

Le président du conseil des ministres, le baron von Lutz en fut bien aise: menacé de congé par Louis II, il pouvait désormais proposer au prince Léopold de mettre le monarque en tutelle, et garder ainsi son poste.

On avait déjà essayé, dans la nuit du 9 au 10 juin, d'arrêter le roi qui séjournait au château de Neuschwanstein, mais les gendarmes et les pompiers des environs appelés en renfort s'y étaient opposés. Une seconde tentative par la dite « commission de capture » venue de Munich fut plus heureuse. Le roi se laissa arrêter sans résistance et emmener vers une voiture. Il demanda il est vrai au chef médical de l'entreprise, le fort réputé Dr. Gudden (et les Bavarois furent plus tard nombreux à se demander si un aliéné mental parle ainsi) « Comment pouvez-vous me déclarer malade mental? Vous ne m'avez pas vu ni examiné auparavant. »

Louis II arriva le 12 juin à midi au château de Berg, sur le lac de Starnberg avec ses médecins et ses surveillants. Le lendemain, jour de la Pentecôte, en fin d'après-midi, il était mort.

Vers 18.30 heures ou 18.45 heures, il avait quitté le château où il était alors interné en compagnie du Dr. Gudden pour faire une promenade. Vers 22.30 heures on trouva les cadavres des deux hommes dans le lac à vingt, vingt-cinq pieds de la rive.

Les circonstances de cette mort n'ont pas été élucidées jusqu'ici. Les discussions vont bon train mais le mystère demeure.

Le roi voulait-il fuir et le Dr. Gudden l'en aurait-il empêché? On dit que Sissi, sa cousine, aurait projeté de l'enlever pour le cacher au Tyrol et que des voitures se tenaient prêtes à quelques endroits à l'extérieur du parc. Le roi voulant fuir aurait-il étranglé le petit Dr. Gudden avant de succomber à une crise cardiaque? L'idée que

König Ludwig auf dem Balkon des Thronsaals von Schloß Neuschwanstein, Ölgemälde von Ferdinand Leeke.

King Ludwig on the balcony of the throne room at Neuschwanstein Castle. Oil painting by Ferdinand Leeke.

Le souverain sur le balcon de la Salle du trône de Neuschwanstein. Peinture à l'huile de Ferdinand Leeke.

Seite 82: Otto, der geisteskranke Bruder König Ludwigs, mit Wärtern.

Page 82: Otto, King Ludwig's mentally ill brother, with his nursing attendants.

Page 82: Othon, le frère aliéné de Louis II, et ses surveillants.

dert. Bei einem zweiten Versuch war die aus München angereiste sogenannte „Fangkommission" erfolgreicher. Der König ließ sich, ohne Widerstand zu leisten, festnehmen und zu einem bereitstehenden Wagen geleiten. Den medizinischen Leiter des Unternehmens, den hochangesehenen Dr. Gudden fragte er aber (und viele Bayern fragten sich später, ob so ein geistig verwirrter Mensch spricht): „Wie können sie mich für geisteskrank erklären? Sie haben mich ja vorher gar nicht gesehen und untersucht."

Am Mittag des 12. Juni war der König mit seinen Ärzten und Bewachern in Schloß Berg am Starnberger See eingetroffen, am Spätnachmittag des darauf folgenden Tages, des Pfingstsonntags, war er tot: Um 18.30 oder 18.45 Uhr verließ er zusammen mit Dr. Gudden sein in eine Irrenanstalt umfunktioniertes Schloß zu einem Spaziergang im Park, um 22.30 Uhr fand man zwanzig bis fünfundzwanzig Fuß vom Ufer entfernt die Leichen der beiden Männer im See treibend.

Die Umstände dieses Todes sind ein großes, immer wieder diskutiertes und doch bis heute nicht gelöstes Rätsel. Wollte der König fliehen und wurde daran von Dr. Gudden gehindert? Die Cousine Sisi, so heißt es, habe eine Entführung Ludwigs nach Tirol vorbereitet und außerhalb des Schloßparks an einigen Stellen Wagen für diese Aktion bereitstellen lassen. Hat der König bei diesem Fluchtversuch den kleinen Dr. Gudden erwürgt und dann selbst einen Herzschlag erlitten? Diese Vorstellung – ihr König ein Mörder – ist den vielen Königstreuen unerträglich. Oder ist der Wittelsbacher,

Oben | Above | Ci-dessus: Dr. Bernhard von Gudden.

Links: Prinzregent Luitpold, seit 1886 „des Königreichs Bayern Verweser".

Left: Prince Regent Luitpold, from 1886 "administrator of the Kingdom of Bavaria".

A gauche: Le prince-régent Léopold, « administrateur du royaume de Bavière » depuis 1886.

Seite 85: Eine der letzten Aufnahmen König Ludwigs, um 1883.

Page 85: A late picture of King Ludwig, c. 1883.

Page 85 : Une des dernières photographies de Louis II, vers 1883.

König Ludwig II.

Das Deutsche Vaterland.

III. Jahrg. 1886.

Humoristisch-satyrisches Wochenblatt mit tragischen Stationen.

Das „Deutsche Vaterland" erscheint jeden Mittwoch Morgens 6 Uhr.

Preis des Blattes: vierteljährig 90 Pfg. inklusive Postzuschlag.

Herausgeber: L. M. Lindner. Redakteur: Hermann Lindner (Hans Linden).

Redaktion und Expedition: Schäfflerstraße 8.

Postexpeditionen und Postboten nehmen Bestellungen an.

„Inserate" werden die vierspaltige Petitzeile oder deren Raum zu 15 Pfg. berechnet.

München, 20. Juni **Nr. 26.** Sonntag.

Leben und Tod.

Die Auffindung der Königs-Leiche.

König Ludwig II. † in Berg.

Die rätselhaften Umstände, unter denen König Ludwig im Starnberger See den Tod fand, haben von Anfang an die Phantasie der Menschen beschäftigt. Sie sind auch heute noch Anlaß zu vielfältigen Spekulationen.

The mysterious circumstances surrounding King Ludwig's death in Lake Starnberg exercised people's imaginations from the beginning and continue to give rise to much speculation today.

Les circonstances mystérieuses dans lesquelles le roi mourut dans le lac de Starnberg n'ont jamais cessé d'alimenter l'imagination populaire. Aujourd'hui encore elles font l'objet de nombreuses spéculations.

König Ludwig im Ornat des Hubertusritterordens, aufgebahrt in der Residenz-Hofkapelle. In der rechten Hand hält er einen Strauß weißen Jasmin, den Kaiserin Elisabeth für ihn gepflückt hat.

King Ludwig in the regalia of the Order of the Knights of St Hubertus, lying in state in the royal chapel at the Munich residence. In his right hand he holds a posy of white jasmine picked for him by the Empress Elisabeth.

Le roi de Bavière qui porte l'habit de cérémonie de l'ordre des Chevaliers de Saint-Hubert est mis en bière dans la chapelle de la résidence royale. Dans la main droite, il tient un bouquet de jasmin blanc que lui a cueilli l'impératrice Elisabeth.

whisk him away. Did the king strangle the diminutive Dr Gudden during the attempted escape and then himself die of a heart attack? The king's many loyal followers find this idea – that their king is a murderer – intolerable. Or did the Wittelsbach scion, an excellent swimmer, drown? This is just as inconceivable as the absurd idea put forward by Philipp Count of Eulenburg, the Prussian ambassadorial secretary, that Ludwig had "forcibly held himself underwater". Or perhaps the king was shot, as has repeatedly been claimed. There is even (allegedly) proof of this: the waistcoat that Ludwig was wearing on that day had a bullet hole in the back, although this piece of evidence can no longer be subjected to analysis because it was destroyed by fire in 1947 or 1948.

And then there is the "testimony" of the king's personal fisherman, Jakob Lidl, who was at the heart of these tragic events, and who said decades after the monarch's death: "Three years after the king's death I was made to swear an oath that I would never say certain things – not to my wife, not on my deathbed, and not to any priest… The state has undertaken to look after my family if anything should happen to me in either peace time or war." Jakob Lidl kept to his oath for as long as he lived, never telling anyone what he knew. But he did write down some notes, which were found after his death. According to these, he had hidden behind bushes with his boat, waiting for the king, in order to row him out into the lake, where escape helpers were already waiting. "As the king stepped up to his boat and put one foot in it, a shot rang out from the bank, apparently killing him on the spot, for the king fell across the bow of the boat." Scared to death and despairing of what to do, Lidl had then shoved the dead monarch into the water and rowed panic-struck back to his cottage, where he crept into his bed, sobbing and weeping.

Many irreconcilable contradictions, and many rumours. But Bavarians have remained true to Ludwig. They have adorned their houses with pictures of him, founded King Ludwig associations, erected some thirty-five monuments and memorials – five of them in Munich alone, the city so little loved by the king – and still light commemorative fires on his birthday up in the mountains. Weighty biographies have been devoted to the monarch, numerous poems have been composed about him, he has appeared in folk dramas, and has "starred" in the famous Munich Studio Theatre in a play

leur roi puisse être un meurtrier est insupportable à ses fidèles. Ou bien, Louis II, excellent nageur au demeurant, se serait-il noyé en voulant fuir? C'est aussi peu concevable que la supposition absurde émise par le secrétaire de l'Ambassade prussienne Philipp comte de Eulenburg, selon laquelle le roi « se serait enfoncé sous l'eau à dessein ».

Ou bien a-t-on peut-être abattu le roi comme on n'a jamais cessé de l'affirmer? Il en existait (paraît-il) même une preuve: le dos de la veste que Louis II portait ce jour-là aurait été troué par une balle, mais impossible d'examiner cette pièce à conviction, elle a été brûlée en 1947 ou 1948.

Et reste encore le pêcheur attitré du roi, Jakob Lidl, qui aida à repêcher les corps et qui déclara, des dizaines d'années plus tard: «Trois ans après la mort du roi, j'ai dû jurer de ne pas révéler certaines choses. Ni à ma femme, ni sur mon lit de mort, ni au prêtre… l'Etat s'est engagé à subvenir aux besoins de ma famille, si quelque chose devait m'arriver. »

Jakob Lidl a tenu parole sa vie durant, mais s'il n'a raconté à âme qui vive ce qu'il savait, il s'est confié au papier, et ses notes ont été trouvées après sa mort. Dissimulé avec son embarcation derrière des buissons, il aurait attendu le roi pour l'emmener sur le lac où se trouvaient ceux qui l'aideraient à fuir. « Le roi s'approcha de la barque, et il avait déjà un pied à l'intérieur, quand un coup de feu éclata sur la rive, le roi fut touché et mourut manifestement sur-le-champ, car il tomba en travers de la barque. » Désespéré et mort de peur, Lidl aurait alors poussé le cadavre du roi dans l'eau et, pris de panique, il se serait réfugié dans sa petite maison, se blottissant sous ses draps en sanglotant.

Que s'est-il vraiment passé le 13 juin 1886? Impossible d'éclaircir les nombreuses contradictions, les bruits courent. Les Bavarois sont restés fidèles à la mémoire de leur roi. Ils ont accroché son portrait dans leurs maisons, créé des associations du Roi Louis, édifié dans les trente-cinq monuments et places commémoratives – dont cinq rien qu'à Munich, la ville mal aimée – et, le jour de son anniversaire, ils allument encore des brasiers commémoratifs sur les montagnes.

Des biographies volumineuses ont été consacrées à Louis II, des poèmes ont chanté sa gloire, on lui donne des rôles dans le théâtre populaire, et la célèbre Kammerspiele de Munich présente une pièce traitant de sa

Der Andrang war so groß, daß man am 19.
Juni 1886 den Weg des Trauerzuges von der
Residenz zur Michaelskirche erheblich ver-
längern mußte.

On 19 June 1886, so many people crowded the
route of the funeral procession from the residence to St Michael's Church that it had to be
extended considerably.

La foule était si dense qu'il fallut allonger de
manière importante le parcours du cortège
funéraire de la Résidence à l'église Saint-
Michel, le 19 juin 1886.

Der Sarkophag des Königs in der Krypta der
Münchner Michaelskirche.

The king's sarcophagus in the crypt of
Munich's Church of St Michael.

Le sarcophage du roi dans la crypte de l'église
Saint-Michel à Munich.

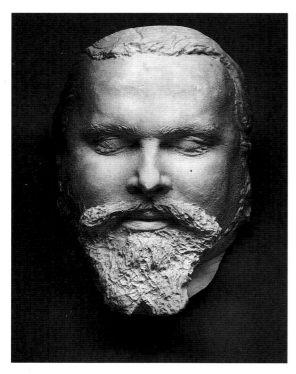

Die Totenmaske Ludwigs II.

The death mask of Ludwig II.

Le masque funéraire de Louis II.

Schloß Berg am Starnberger See.

Berg Castle on Lake Starnberg.

Le château de Berg sur le lac de Starnberg.

ein exzellenter Schwimmer, bei der Flucht ertrunken? Das ist ebensowenig vorstellbar wie die vom preußischen Gesandtschaftssekretär Philipp Graf zu Eulenburg geäußerte absurde Vermutung, Ludwig habe „sich gewaltsam unter das Wasser gedruckt".

Oder hat man den König vielleicht doch erschossen, wie immer wieder behauptet wurde? Dafür gab es (angeblich) sogar einen Beweis: Die Weste, die Ludwig an jenem Tag getragen hat, wies im Rücken ein Einschußloch auf, doch eine Untersuchung dieses Beweisstückes ist nicht mehr möglich, es wurde 1947 oder 1948 verbrannt.

Und da ist dann immer noch der kgl. Leibfischer Jakob Lidl, der bei der Bergung der Leichen eine wichtige Rolle spielte und Jahrzehnte nach dem Tod des Monarchen sagte: „Ich habe drei Jahre nach dem Tod des Königs einen Eid schwören müssen, daß ich verschiedene Dinge nicht sagen würde. Nicht meiner Frau, und nicht auf dem Sterbebette und auch nicht dem Priester... Der Staat hat sich dabei verpflichtet, danach für meine Familie zu sorgen, wenn mir im Krieg oder Frieden etwas Menschliches passieren sollte."

Jakob Lidl hat wohl zeitlebens den Eid gehalten und niemandem erzählt, was er wußte. Doch er hat sich Notizen darüber gemacht, die nach seinem Tod gefunden wurden. Danach habe er mit seinem Boot, hinter Büschen versteckt, auf den König gewartet, um ihn aufzunehmen und in den See hinauszurudern, wo Fluchthelfer bereits warteten. „Wie der König nun auf seinen Kahn zugeschritten und einen Fuß bereits in das Boot gesetzt habe, sei vom Ufer ein Schuß gefallen, der den König offensichtlich sogleich getötet habe, denn dieser sei quer über den Bug des Bootes gefallen. In seiner Verzweiflung und Todesangst habe Lidl dann den toten König ins Wasser geschoben und sei in panischer Angst zurück zu seinem Häuschen gerudert. Dort habe er sich schluchzend und weinend in sein Bett verkrochen."

Seite 91: Ein Kreuz markiert die Stelle im See, wo die Leichen von König Ludwig und Dr. von Gudden gefunden wurden.

Page 91: A cross marks the place where the bodies of King Ludwig and Dr von Gudden were found.

Page 91 : Une croix désigne l'endroit où furent découverts les corps inanimés de Louis II et du Dr. von Gudden.

Viele unlösbare Widersprüche, mancherlei Gerüchte. Die Bayern haben ihrem König aber auch später ihre Liebe und Treue bewahrt. Sie schmückten Wohnungen mit seinem Bild, gründeten König-Ludwig-Vereine, errichteten wohl an die fünfunddreißig Denkmäler und Gedenkstätten – fünf davon allein in München, dieser vom König so wenig geliebten Stadt – und zünden an seinem Geburtstag noch immer auf den Bergen Gedenkfeuer an.

Dem König wurden gewichtige Biographien gewidmet, man dichtete viele Reime auf ihn, ließ ihn in Volksstücken auftreten und zeigte in den berühmten Münchner Kammerspielen ein Stück über das Ende des Märchenkönigs im See, mit Peter Pasetti als König Ludwig.

Der triumphale Einzug in die modernen Massenmedien erfolgte 1955, als O. W. Fischer in dem Helmut-Käutner-Film „Ludwig II. Glanz und Elend eines Königs" das Ludwig-Bild von Generationen prägte. Der Ludwigfilm von Luchino Visconti aus dem Jahre 1972 (mit Helmut Berger als König Ludwig) wurde ebenfalls ein großer Publikumserfolg. Der ein Jahr später uraufgeführte Film „Ludwig. Requiem für einen jungfräulichen König" von Hans-Jürgen Syberberg blieb hingegen ein Fall für Cineasten.

Inzwischen plant man zur Ankurbelung des Tourismusgeschäfts und zum Ärger wie zum Entsetzen vieler Ludwig-Anhänger im Schatten von Neuschwanstein ein Ludwig-Musical mit einem eigens dafür zu errichtenden Theater.

Die langen Jahrzehnte, in denen die von Ludwig II. in Auftrag gegebenen Schlösser und deren kunsthandwerkliche Ausgestaltung mit Spott bedacht wurden, sind lange vergangen. Spätestens seit der großen, phantasievoll inszenierten Ausstellung „König Ludwig II. und die Kunst" in der Münchner Residenz (1968) hat sich die Einschätzung des Monarchen verändert, so daß zehn Jahre später auch das Londoner Victoria and Albert Museum sowie das Cooper-Hewitt Museum in New York mit der Ausstellung „Designs for the Dream King" auf unerwartet großes Interesse traf.

Der König ist tot und wird noch lange leben.

about the lakeside gate of the fairytale king, with Peter Pasetti playing Ludwig. He has even made a triumphal entry into the modern mass media. In 1955 O.W. Fischer moulded the Ludwig image for generations in Helmut Käutner's film "Ludwig II. Glory and Misery of a King". Luchino Visconti's Ludwig film of 1972 (with Helmut Berger as King Ludwig) was likewise highly popular and influential. By contrast, Hans-Jürgen Syberberg's film "Ludwig. Requiem for a Virgin King", premiered a year later, has remained something for cinema buffs. Now plans are afoot, to the annoyance and disgust of many people living in the shadow of Neuschwanstein, to create a Ludwig musical for tourists, to be performed in a purpose-built theatre.

The many decades in which the castles and exquisitely crafted decorations commissioned by Ludwig II were laughed out of court, the times of aesthetic underestimation and scorn have long since passed. At the latest since the extensive and, imaginatively mounted exhibition "King Ludwig II and his Art", held in the royal capital Munich in 1968, the verdict on the monarch has changed, so that ten years later the exhibition "Designs for the Dream King", held at the Victoria and Albert Museum in London and at the Cooper-Hewitt Museum in New York, met with great interest – far more than was expected.

The king is dead, but also very much alive – long may he live!

disparition avec Peter Pasetti dans le rôle de Louis II.

Il a fait son entrée triomphale dans les médias modernes en 1955 avec le « Louis II » de Helmut Käutner: l'acteur O. W. Fischer forgea une image de Louis II qui marquera des générations de spectateurs. Le film de Luchino Visconti tourné en 1972 avec Helmut Berger dans le rôle principal aura un succès similaire. En revanche, le film « Louis. Requiem pour un roi vierge » de Hans-Jürgen Syberberg, sorti un an plus tard, restera réservé aux cinéphiles.

Aujourd'hui on envisage pour des raisons touristiques, et au grand dam de ceux qui vivent à l'ombre de Neuschwanstein, la création d'un musical Ludwig avec un théâtre conçu à cet effet.

On a longtemps raillé les châteaux de Louis II et leur décoration – est-ce un hasard si c'est à Munich que le mot « kitsch » apparaît, preuve à l'appui, pour la première fois après 1870 – mais le temps du dédain et du mépris est révolu depuis longtemps. L'idée que l'on se faisait du monarque a changé, au moins depuis la grande exposition « Le Roi Louis II et l'art » mise en scène avec talent dans la résidence de Munich (1968), ce qui fait que dix ans plus tard l'exposition « Designs for the Dream King » présentée au Victoria and Albert Museum de Londres ainsi qu'au Cooper-Hewitt Museum de New York a connu un succès inattendu.

Le Roi est mort, et longtemps il vivra.

Die Urne mit dem Herz des Königs in der Gnadenkapelle zu Altötting.

The urn containing the king's heart in the Chapel of our Gracious Lady in Altötting.

L'urne contenant le cœur du roi, conservée dans la chapelle de la Grâce près de Altötting.

Szene mit Klaus Kinski und O.W. Fischer als
Ludwig II. in dem von Helmut Käutner 1955
gedrehten Film „Ludwig II. Glanz und Elend
eines Königs".

A scene from the 1955 movie by Helmut Käutner about Ludwig II, with Klaus Kinski and
O.W. Fischer as the royal personage.

Scène du film « Louis II » réalisé en 1955 par
Helmut Käutner, avec Klaus Kinski et O. W.
Fischer dans le rôle du roi.

Regisseur Luchino Visconti mit Romy Schneider als Elisabeth von Österreich und Helmut Berger als Ludwig bei den Dreharbeiten zu seinem Film „Ludwig II." (1972).

Director Luchino Visconti with Romy Schneider as Elisabeth of Austria and Helmut Berger as Ludwig, during filming of the movie "Ludwig II" (1972).

Le réalisateur Luchino Visconti avec Romy Schneider dans le rôle d'Elisabeth d'Autriche et Helmut Berger dans celui de Louis II sur le tournage de « Louis II » (1972).

Szene aus demselben Film: Der König ist tot aufgefunden worden.

A scene from the same movie: The king is discovered dead.

Une scène du film: on vient de découvrir le corps du roi.